MW00711120

DUNES REVIEW

EDITORIAL BOARD

SENIOR EDITORS   Teresa Scollon
                              Jennifer Yeatts

EDITORIAL SUPPORT   Kelli Fitzpatrick

READERS   Chris Giroux
                             Paul Oh
                             Emma Smith

FOUNDING EDITOR   Anne-Marie Oomen

PATRONS

John Flesher   Susan Odgers
Tanya Muzumdar   Anne-Marie Oomen
National Writers Series   Teresa Scollon
            Patricia Trentacoste

COVER IMAGE : *Fiddlehead* by Diane Carr

Aluminum, Acrylics, Sand. 41"x 20"x 10". Image courtesy of the artist. The artwork was given to Dennos Museum Center at Northwestern Michigan College in Traverse City, Michigan, as a gift in memory of Daniel Carr.

DUNES REVIEW

VOLUME 25 ISSUE 2

FALL/WINTER 2021

CONTENTS

Editors' Notes

The cover image of Diane Carr's sculpture *Fiddlehead* makes me think of spring in all its vibrant color. It's winter now, of course, and I have no wish to escape it. I love winter. I need this quiet time for rest and reflection before spring comes with its changes. Underneath the snow, mud, or whatever it is we're going to get this winter, the fiddlehead is lying dormant, getting ready to show itself. That's a motif that runs through some of the work in this issue: things that lie just out of our view. It might be unrealized potential, or an unrecognized identity, or memories evoked when we look at something else. It might be the emergence of disease or dis-ease. It might be how we learn how to draw on our hidden strengths when needed. I spent some time on the phone with artist Diane Carr, listening to how she works with the material and lets it speak to her, lets it tell her what form it should take. The process of listening closely and paying attention to what must emerge is so essential that I hardly know how to describe it. But I want to be reminded of it. And I'm so grateful to read the work of these artists who are doing just that as writers. I hope you enjoy these pieces. Thank you, as always, for your support and attention.

— *Teresa Scollon*

Our bodies: they betray us. In youth we dare them to stretch, to balance, to reach, in general to perform for our imaginations on command. Our bodies, still capable of pushing boundaries, are resilient. Until they aren't. Eventually, they defy the commands. And we are puzzled, bereft, dismayed that our physical forms do not obey the desires of our intellect. Maybe, for some of us, it's the observation of others near to us that illuminates that bodily frailty. For some of us it is painfully evident in our own bodies. Throughout this issue, intellect wrestles with physical realities, like the heart's desire to be near loved ones in the midst of pressures to be distant, even if it is for the greater good.

Impermanence makes things, and people, precious. The more temporal something is, the greater value it represents. The pieces in this issue lift up many of those treasures, from the briefest of moments visiting a friend in the driveway to fishing with an aging father. *In the future, light comes from the past*, Catherine Turnbull writes, *and I am turning back to look.* Dear readers, let's look together and trust those fleeting, precious moments to shine their light into our collective future.

— *Jennifer Yeatts*

Danielle Johnson
DEAR NATALIE DIAZ—

I am lonely   which is a pathetic way
of saying Arizona is too big for me and I feel so
incredibly small in it

I tried to google people to meet by putting
in symptoms of my illness (loneliness) I searched:

cactus are boring
why won't the sun stop hating me

I couldn't believe any poets could live here
which is selfish and assumes that I am the only
person who takes on this poetic work

All I learned was Emma Stone's parents
live near me   I'm sure they're nice people
but I don't really care about them   I learned you
lived here by listening to poets on interviews

I was making dinner and doing dishes. I've
run out of poets to call. Every poet I know
keeps transforming into a homemaker   a mother
they are working towards their final form

I know I am not the only one writing you but
I have found myself addressing you in my head
in the same way I sometimes pray to God   it's an
impossibility but still a hope that someone

Out there is listening   am I the only one on the
planet alone?   I know that is a stupid question.

Do you know about God at all? Sometimes he
would send people to the desert   They would
never just give up and die. They'd find shade trees

or imagine rushing waters   where there was valley
they imagined a possibility outside of their own

I think you could teach me something about this. My final
form has nothing to do with being a mother and will
never be cool on the internet. I need the kind of help that
my students ask for.

what can i do   an email title read
can you point me in the direction of success

Bailey Quinn
SELF-PORTRAIT AS PANIC ATTACKS

I eat a can of Spaghetti-Os, not
because my shelves are bare or

because they cost a dollar and most
of my paycheck went to bills from

my last psych eval, but because they
taste like summer, when Mom stayed

home running through sprinklers
with me, her laugh filled the yard,

warmed the afternoon rain, and I
asked what was for dinner. She said,

"you choose." Our laminate counter
cool under my thighs, I watched Mom

stir a can of just the O's because "Lord
knows what's in the meatballs." On

a soft velvet couch in my own house
decades later, after four panic attacks

shook my body, carving my chest
like a can-opener, I sob over my bowl,

methodically count each meatball,
blearily set them aside on a paper plate.

Natalie Welber
SHOWER REQUIEM

I drop the soap
and laugh
and cry

watch it try to float
and no one knows
our joke lost weeks ago

no laughter through the door
like on so many nights before
so many soaps slipping

through slick fingers
plunk! from the floor
sometimes you can't hold on anymore

the drain is clogged
and soapy suds
drown out my toes

which shrivel
saturated
slurping like that sponge

pulled across limp lips
desperately deparching
a spirit departing

my body will
probably
kill me too

Alexis Newton
DOWN THE HALL

after Warsan Shire and Dorianne Laux

Imagine the bathroom sink is the last thing you see.
Imagine the shine of water laminated bronze,
the drip of rain from cloud to lake.
Imagine the way your mother knocks at the door,
the half-empty tube of toothpaste
wrinkled like bath towels curled in the corner.
Imagine the dried film on the lotion bottle
and the way your last seconds look in the mirror.
Imagine feeling the December ice on the tile,
realizing your last touch of warmth is the grout.
Imagine the patter of the shower against the walls
and the way the jarred window lets the wind infiltrate
the silence. Imagine the clock on the wall, the ticking
that was once more than a sentence, that reminded you of
what it means to hear breath.

What it means to hear breath
that was once more than a sentence, that reminded you of
the silence. Imagine the clock on the wall, the ticking
and the way the jarred window lets the wind infiltrate.
Imagine the patter of the shower against the walls,
realizing your last touch of warmth is the grout.
Imagine feeling the December ice on the tile,
and the way your last seconds look in the mirror.
Imagine the dried film on the lotion bottle
wrinkled like bath towels curled in the corner,
the half-empty tube of toothpaste.
Imagine the way your mother knocks at the door,
the drip of rain from cloud to lake.
Imagine the shine of water laminated bronze.
Imagine the bathroom sink is the last thing you see.

Bailey Quinn
HYPOMANIA

I scrub the baseboards
over and
over and

the dirt won't come off
spreads like freckles

on a face branded
behind my eyelids,
I lay in bed next
to my husband
naked, I scrub

thoughts
out of my brain
skin off my bones —
too much, keeping me
together, *right*

over there is where
I buried myself, under the
diseased rosebush outside
our bedroom window

it's cramped, cool
rain spills down
from the gutter.

Catherine Turnbull
ONE MOMENT WITH YOUR MANIA

I was learning to split wood,
in the side yard, shards of bark
riddled around the stump
in shades of umber.
I was drawn to the axe, the lift, the fall—bright thump of it.
The next time the phone rang it would be bad news
but she could not have known I feared that.
She said she was happy,
though I heard something else.
It's hard to remember with experience in the way.
It's easy to remember the pieces I could not split,
the awkward hit, the tumbling steel weight.
I found the aptly named knots
interesting, how they resisted.
I emptied one pile to create another.
In the future, light comes from the past,
and I am turning back to look.
I stood on the scraps of tree skin,
hard but crumbling, holding the hard axe,
her voice something I was watching.
What I didn't know wasn't in the axe
or the wood that would not give way;
what I didn't know wasn't in the bark-strewn soil.

Corinna Schulenberg
THE CHICKEN WAS A DINOSAUR

the chicken swears it once was a dinosaur and ruled
over creation. I'm on vacation so I let myself get fooled

and say *go on.* the chicken leads me to the bushes flush
with raspberries, pecks them raw, calls it blood. A rush

of savage possibilities, a muddy river of ash and water,
a homemade cave to summon the dead, a daughter

with grasshopper legs, who bellows for more life, even after
a heap of happens; this list I rattle off to my new master,

the one of swift beak, stilt step, and jiggle crown, and say
this is what I have to offer. teach me all your dinosaur ways,

for I too would rule, I too would stab the earth with a mouth
that too often kisses when it should strike, too often doubts

its own creation. the chicken considers me with avian
inscrutability, clucks, *tell me the names of all the men*

who've hurt you, and your throat will reveal if you're ready.
my tongue, an executioner, collects the list, grim, steady,

until I see her, my daughter, eyes wide as blown dandelions,
wondering how the arms that an hour ago had set her flying

are now so full of wound, of weed, of bitter, of snake.
the chicken waits to see what kind of choice I'll make.

a magician of old, I vanish the wounds with a flick of wrist,
swallow down the list, smile, and let the tale persist

that I am right as rain. the sky tucks away her reckonings,
and the chicken is a chicken again, ridiculously pecking

in all the wrong places. *carry me, mama.* I lift her up.
I hold her close. we feed the chicken from a little cup.

Tuuli Qin-Terrill
HOW TO FILLET A FISH

First, do not pity the subject. It is dead, cold, rotting on your cutting board. Bow, or nod or curtsy. It is only the polite thing to do. After all, you will soon slit its belly. Pick up your knife. It'd better be clean and long and sharp. If not, you're doing this all wrong. Breathe in. Whisper *Salmo salar* under your breath; that's real Atlantic salmon for you. Breathe out. Wait, did you wash your hands? Wash your hands. Mr. Ken will not sign your check if you forget again. Return to the block. Bow again. Line up your blade on the fish's jawline, just behind the gills but in front of its ventral fins. Slice down until you hear the backbone creak, feel the slightest resistance. Do not be lawless with your tool; you are not a butcher but an artist. Do not mind the blood on your fingers or the slime under your nails, just as a painter doesn't mind the paint in their hair or the sculptor doesn't mind the clay on their apron. Accept that it comes with the trade. This is messy grace.

Breathe again. Turn your knife horizontal. Using the backbone as your guide, slide your knife slowly towards the tail. Don't cut your hand. The hospital doesn't want to see you again, Mr. Ken doesn't want to meet with the Department of Agriculture and Rural Development again or pay for the stitches, and you don't want to explain to your mother why you love your job. Not again. She sees you come home with the scent of fish clinging to your clothes and scales sprinkled in your hair. She pounds the knots out of your shoulders, tells you it's not too late to go back and finish one of the college degrees you never completed in architecture, in global commerce, in philosophy, in anything. You shake your head because she just doesn't get it. She can't smell the salt of the ocean, hear the slap of a fifty-pound salmon on your block, feel the weight of the carver in your calloused hands, or see the striated, orange flesh of a freshly filleted salmon carcass. You really don't want to try and explain to your mother why you love your job. That if you could, you'd stand at that cutting block for all eternity.

But honestly, you're barely scraping by and Mr. Ken talked to you just last week about meeting quota. The scars on your hands keep multiplying and your arthritis makes it harder and harder to hold the blade with grace. Your relationship with your mother is strained. She refuses to attend the cocktail parties thrown by the parents of lawyers and surgeons and even aspiring actors. Because what is she supposed to talk about when her only child's best friends are a sharp knife and a dead fish? Maybe if she hasn't given up on suggesting college, this time you'll finally realize that all she wants is the best for you and your future, that she won't be around your whole life, that you can't be a fishmonger forever.

Now, if you haven't broken the salmon's backbone, or cut your finger, or accidentally sneezed but forgot to cover your mouth, flip the fish over. Rinse and repeat. Hour after hour. Keep up the dance until you pierce your skin and see red, until Mr. Ken kicks you out because he doesn't want to pay you overtime, until the ocean runs out of fish.

Paul Maxbauer
SMALL CONSOLATIONS

One week after his parents' big argument, the boy sat on the back porch throwing a jackknife into the scarred wood of the bottom step. Wearing dark framed-glasses and short-cropped hair that gave him the look of a young scientist, he was dressed in jeans, sneakers, and a blue t-shirt that read *Detroit Tigers* on the front.

Home was a small city in northern Michigan, but the boy had never visited Detroit, had never seen a Tigers game in person. An avid fan, he had to be content reading the box scores in the local newspaper and listening to games broadcast on the radio, sometimes falling asleep to Ernie Harwell's melodic voice calling the play-by-play of late night games from the West Coast. Later, when he was fast asleep, his dad would slip into his room and turn off the radio.

At age fourteen, the boy was starting to grow into his tall, lanky frame, with big hands that helped him effortlessly grip and throw baseballs and footballs. He was also good at helping around the house, routinely mowing the lawn, raking leaves, and shoveling snow. He even worked for Mrs. Brown next door, helping her weed, transplant flowers, and spread mulch on her extensive gardens.

With his earnings, he'd opened a savings account at the credit union. The feeling of independence, of being able to buy a new baseball or fishing lure whenever he wanted, felt good. The first thing he'd purchased was a copy of *The Trout Fisherman's Bible*, which he'd read from cover to cover and kept on his nightstand. He dreamed about someday fishing the great rivers of America, like the Yellowstone and the Madison.

He figured he would get yelled at if his dad could see all the knife marks in the porch step, but his dad wasn't home. He retrieved the knife and threw it again, aiming for a smooth knot near the front edge of the step, feeling satisfied when he hit it dead center. It was a sign, he told himself, that everything would be all right.

A week ago he'd heard his parents arguing, heard the harsh words, the dinner plates smashing on the floor, his mother shouting, "It's either her or me, and what about the kids? Have you forgotten them?" Then came the slamming of the door and his mother's tears.

Later, after his father left, he saw her staring out the window, a faraway look in her eyes.

His father had a temper. The boy was occasionally afraid of him, like he was afraid of a sharp clap of thunder. But in the good times his father taught him how to fish and played catch with him, helping him gain the skills and confidence he needed to pitch in the summer baseball league. He wanted his dad home, wanted his parents to be happy like other parents. Was that too much to ask?

Yesterday was the last day of school, today the start of summer vacation. With his lunch finished and his morning chores complete, he decided to ride his bike to the creek for some fishing. He closed his jackknife, shoved it in his pocket, and gathered his fishing gear. His mother called to him as he was leaving the yard, "Be home before dinner. I could use some help. And bring home some trout! Your father will like that if he comes home."

If he comes home, that was the question. The boy was tired of pondering the outcome and he felt the heaviness of worrying, the aching in his heart. As he walked through the garage to get his bike, he picked up a hatchet lying on the work bench. Resting on sawhorses was his dad's prized *Old Town* canoe. Swinging three times with the hatchet, he struck the canoe, leaving open wounds in the canvas-wood bottom. *See how you like that, Dad, next time you go canoeing*, he thought. Feeling weighed down with emotion, he swung onto his bike and rode out of the yard.

At the creek, carrying a fishing pole and a wicker creel slung across his shoulders, he crossed one bridge and then another, following the stream as it coursed through the city neighborhoods. He liked to stand on the bank, on the upstream side of a bridge, and drift a red worm or a grasshopper down under, letting it move naturally with the current, waiting for a strike.

It was a dark, cool, watery world underneath the bridge. The air smelled of rank green grass, decaying leaves, and mint, and the boy liked it. He liked everything about fishing. He liked the sense of timelessness, the progress of a normal day being suspended, and the thrill of a solid strike, knowing that, for one glorious moment, everything wonderful in the world was at the end of his line.

He fished with the sunshine warming his neck and arms, listening to the calls of birds, the buzzing insects, and traffic on the streets. Standing a few feet below street level, with only a limited view of passersby, he felt hidden from the world. He had nowhere to be but where he was, along the creek. All he wanted was to focus on where a trout might be holding, the next cast, and the next bite.

After a couple of hours, the creel resting against his hip held four plump brook trout, each one a slippery slab of muscle with dazzling colors: olive backs, flanks speckled with red dots bounded by blue halos, orange fins edged with slashes of white. He thought about staying there all afternoon in that brook trout heaven. If he wanted, he could catch his limit and wile away the time until night fell, but he felt the tug of home.

His father was a truck driver who made local deliveries, so normally he came home at the end of his runs, but now he'd been gone a whole week. His mother, with pursed lips and a stoic face, said little to the boy by way of explanation. She merely asked him to do some extra jobs around the house and help look after his younger brother and sister.

But the boy knew why his father hadn't come home. The idea that his dad had a girlfriend somewhere filled him with confusion and a hurt that did not abate. What would happen to Mom, to all of them, if his dad didn't come home? All the boy could do was mull things over and try to help his mom where he could. He pulled in his line to check the bait, then made another cast. Where the line entered the water, it quivered and moved sideways. He raised the rod tip and was tight to another trout, which made a spirited run for the bottom before tiring and coming to his hand. This made five: a good catch. It was time to go home.

Using the pocketknife, he slit open the bellies of the fish and pulled out the entrails. He scraped all the blood out of the body cavities by running a thumbnail along the spines before rinsing them off in the stream. He then placed them on a bed of wet grass in his creel.

Before getting on his bike, he picked up a smooth, round stone and hefted it. Picking out a tree along the stream bank, he went into his pitching windup, aiming for a bare spot on the tree where the bark had fallen away. But he over-threw, lunging into the pitch with all his might, the stone sailing far off the mark and across the creek, him nearly falling off the steep bank and into the mud. Wow, that's overkill, he thought. No reason to throw that hard. He chose another stone, calmed himself and pitched again.

Bullseye. He hit it right where he wanted, a good rehearsal for tomorrow's game. He had to remember to keep his normal motion, stay balanced, and throw strikes, just like Dad taught him. If he could do those things, he knew he would be okay.

He leaped onto his bike with renewed energy, but as the satisfaction of hitting his target diminished, his pedaling slowed. He shouldn't get his hopes up. His dad wouldn't be there. It would be eight days tomorrow; why would he show up now? Feelings of injury and anger overtook him, and remorse for ruining the canoe. He took a deep breath and haltingly exhaled, a shuddering that felt like crying.

He kept pedaling, the slow burning inside him settling into something he could manage. He reminded himself that he had a good arm. He'd caught five brook trout worth bringing home. He could be counted on to show up at the game tomorrow.

The sun shone softly in slants of golden light filtering through the maple trees. The air remained warm. He watched the shadows grow longer and heard bees working in neighborhood gardens. School was out, it was summer, and he was pitching tomorrow. That was something.

Deborah Allbritain
DRIVE

It's okay if what
surrounds you
lacks plush, bitters

about unpolished
and uneven
because all

you are up against
now is mainstream,
not a dipping of

extremes, but the
bustle
of a thing heading

north, up the trachea
of California,
a straight

shot which is how
you travel if
there is closure or seizure.

You become
angora, lean out
the window,

steer hard
away as though
you were a sentence

of oncoming speed.
Leave in its wake
your shed

back and shoulders.
Wipe your brow.
Hold to the median,

leave poised
on the brink of open.

Clayne Zollinger
CANNERY ROW BUS STOP

Even the pigeons here look better, Gabi says as we wait
for a bus. *They're so much prettier, their colors are so much*

brighter than the ones in Oakland, I say. *And fatter.* I've
learned a pigeon can tell so much about a city. I look down

at my dirty sneakers, scuffed soles and the beginning of
a hole, and try to pin down just what I might reveal about

the city I am from and what someone might know about
home from my face now. The bus is here now. Pigeons

scatter and the people shuffle off steps onto sidewalk while
we shuffle ourselves up, and I am trying not to give away

too much, trying not to shame myself. My mother would
send me off to school, shooing me out the door saying:

Remember who you are and where you came from, and
I didn't understand what she meant, what sharing a name

meant, what the word legacy meant until later, until I was
sixteen and had my first job interview. *You're the attorney's*

*son? He's a good man; got me out of a sticky situation. Can
you start Monday?* But what can be told about a town by

its possums, rooting in the trash bins behind the trailer
park just beyond city limits or by the carp caught off the

city dock on the Snake (if it can be called a city)? I was
in another town, miles away on my twelfth birthday, when

a stout stranger stopped me in a Mormon church parking
lot, called me by my last name. *You are one, right?* she said.

I married a Zollinger. You look like one. She laughed, asked me
who my father was, as if it told her everything.

Ron Riekki
DIOS, REZO

> *Crows are dropping stones into the oceans. Don't let them.*
> —Jonathan Greenhause, "One Will Devour the Other"

I don't mind the crows dropping their stones into the ocean.
They worked hard for those stones and the ocean is so hungry.
I don't mind the cows dropping their crows into the ocean.
The crows carry stones and so it is just more stones for the ocean.
I don't mind the milkmaids milking those cows as they fly through
the air carrying their crows and stones and oceans. And all the
milkmaids' coworkers and all the call girls who wave on the shore,
with the waves all hungry for more. And more. And I have tried to
pick up a maid who was cleaning up after the milkmaids and instead
the maid picked me up and I was a stone and we flew toward her
home and the ocean? —it had everything it had ever wanted. And I
hope the same for you. Amen.

Emma Karnes
ETHER

I go with my wings to the edge of the earth,
I deliberate faith and the breaking of eggs. Oh, oh,
I moved here against the vacuum of your wanting
for love; I'm continentally-far with these wide-
swooping crows. You're the edge of the earth
falling away from my toes. You're the turquoise planes
of irrational expanse, of total undoing, of goosebumping
belief. Where the stars unroll, winking with power,
(which you futilely want, being also the land), our stars
which you counted on the fingers of your hands.
Was there ever a secret that everyone knew?
Something like that might help me forgive you.

Deirdre Mahoney
TOGETHER AND ALONE

I've been determined to sidestep the crisis and drama associated with Alzheimer's, but I'm coming to understand the pathos exists for a reason. It's real. It's universal, even if it's true what they say: "If you've seen one case of Alzheimer's, you've seen one case of Alzheimer's." Every case of the neurological illness progresses uniquely, yet the universal experience *is* also the universal experience.

My husband's decline has been slow, beginning with an initial diagnosis of Mild Cognitive Impairment (MCI) and then Alzheimer's six years later. MCI isn't a disease; rather, it's a description of symptoms without a definitive explanation. Essentially, it's a let's-wait-and-see statement—a pause before the verdict. What we know now is that in John's case, MCI was actually the early stages of Alzheimer's, but the signs were so subtle and John compensated so well and looked so young that dementia, and Alzheimer's specifically, didn't seem a likely cause. While the turtle pace has been a gift as Alzheimer's goes, it has also misled me. What irony. Alzheimer's has misled me! John's gradual decline left me believing the process would always be slow and gentle enough and that he'd be mostly okay. Mostly himself. That we'd manage well as a couple, indefinitely.

Lately I'm drawn to thinking about the "younger-onset" aspect that gets tagged to John's diagnosis and the unfairness of the added insult. Announcing illness as unfair or as having arrived too soon makes little sense. I know this, but isn't it distressing enough to be greeted with dementia in old age, when the body is busy shutting itself down as it's designed to do?

Subtle signs of a cognitive shift began in 2008 when John wasn't yet sixty. He was fifty-eight, close to my age now. Couldn't the illness have held off ten or fifteen or twenty years? Wouldn't that have been more reasonable? As if any of this can be neatly sorted, comprehended, reasoned.

I consider how, if John's Alzheimer's were to surface now at age 68 instead of 58, we'd still have had time to do plenty of living together as a couple. Maybe we could have enjoyed a period of shared retirement. We could have moved along a bit more collectively, embracing a less-harried pace. While settling into the final chapter, we could have been out in the world, meeting new people, discovering unexplored places together, still talking in depth about complicated things, or even the most routine. Today, our conversations don't go far. I keep things simple and default to pleasant talk. I ask John what he might want or what he might need help with, as in "How about a hot chocolate?" or "You've spent a lot of time with *Junk City*. You ready for some different poetry?" I offer him the Ogden Nash collection my sister sent a few weeks back when I told her he sits and pages through poetry for hours at a time. John responds to my question with a lack of enthusiasm. Good, I think. At least he still knows what he likes and dislikes. No offense to Nash. Nor my thoughtful sister.

Sometimes I theorize the point of John's early-onset is so that I might be of eventual support to others who one day will wake up and realize dementia has hijacked their marriages too. I'll be able to explain what happens and what it's like to live within a mandated type of complacency. I'll say things like this:

Your partner will struggle with every decision, so best to make them all. Avoid providing choices. Order for the two of you at restaurants. Simplify!

Go ahead and label the containers as SOAP and SHAMPOO so to avoid confusion in the shower. Know that eventually labeling won't make a difference.

When inquiring about a GPS tracker for your partner, best to explain up front about the Alzheimer's. Otherwise, the Verizon rep will assume your marriage a pathetic mess and you a contemptible spy.

Even if you remind your husband twice that the recycling bin is the one with the neon-green lid, thirty-five steps later he won't remember.

It's what happens.

❖ ❖ ❖

Our home has begun to feel cramped during these dark winter months in northern Michigan. John and I seem glued to one another, particularly now while I'm on sabbatical leave. Within the confined space, my mind wanders far and wide to all the what-ifs and whys.

Why did we give up on a second child? Why didn't we adopt all those years ago? We talked about it for a while and then stopped. Decision made. Why didn't we travel more when we were younger? Why did I fixate on the mundane? *Did I fixate on the mundane?* Was I a good mother? Was I around enough? We should have created more family traditions. Wasn't that my responsibility?

Although our only child, Jack, loves us immensely and we him, I imagine additional grown children today—daughters—their lives and their partners and babies and chaos and family clamor in the house during holidays. Snapshots appear in my mind from nearly thirty years ago, the time shortly after my father had died. I see all of us—my sisters, sisters-in-law, and me—crowded into the hectic space of my mother's kitchen while supporting strapping toddlers on hips, rocking tiny babies in arms. Did I comprehend the level of comfort we must have provided my mother at the time?

Daughters might text or call me during the week, I surmise. Would they ask my advice? Would we talk about everything and nothing? Maybe they'd find me imposing, difficult, bossy, controlling, and not reach out at all. If I'm going down this road, I should probably consider all the unpleasant possibilities. And then I consider the next chapter, a future where I think about venturing out on my own, seeking new avenues for making a difference, leaving a positive trace. Maybe I'll volunteer for VISTA, become a Big Sister, disappear into a different place and person. But before any of that, I should begin with things closer to home. First, I'll have to adjust to a more solitary existence. I worry about living alone in a quiet house, which is clearly contradictory since I've always gravitated toward solitude and autonomy. But contradictory it is.

And what about household basics? Will I dash home from campus during the lunch hour to walk the dogs? It's safer than walking them in the early morning when I might lose my footing in the dark and slip in the alley or on a sidewalk. Neither pet demonstrates Lassie-like inclinations, so who would help me?

How will I ever manage the autumn yard cleanup on my own with all the leaves and garden clippings? Last summer I taught myself how to mow the lawn with the trusty push mower. Now I know: Anyone can do it!

What about flashlights? John used to keep one in every room, in case of a household emergency, predicaments he always managed.

But when the electricity went out a few weeks ago in the middle of the night, I couldn't locate a single one. How did I even know we were without power? I was asleep and then awake, aware that something wasn't right. For a few moments I was confused and uncertain about what to do. All the while, John slept peacefully, unaware, in bed next to me.

✵✵✵

At the café where I write early in the day, I eavesdrop on conversations around me. I hear a woman my age one table over talking with a friend about the trouble in her marriage. Her husband's always angry, she says. He won't talk to her, so she leaves him notes. The same woman's grown daughter expects her to take on babysitting duties. The woman says her endurance is limited but she's establishing boundaries, something she's never done well before. I want to say to her, "At least you have emotion in your marriage, even if it feels isolating and hurtful. At least you have the welcome noise of grandchildren within easy reach. Be happy. Rejoice!"

At another table I hear a man John's age talk about his father who has Alzheimer's. Fortunately, the man says, they've found a woman to help out. She comes to the house to make certain the man with Alzheimer's doesn't do "stupid things." Without her, he'd need assisted living. This setup is better, the man explains. I want to interrupt him and say, "No setup is better."

John still asks, "How can I help?" Of course, I have to supervise every last thing I ask of him, but, still, it's nice he asks. Last night while watching television, Zelda, our little Havanese dog, pawed at the back door to go outside. Without me even glancing his way, John jumped up, acting on cue. So considerate, I thought. That's how you can help. You can still surprise me by responding to a paw at the back door. Several minutes later, though, I heard scraping along the walkway. John was outside in the night shoveling the falling snow. No parka or fleece to guard against the biting cold. "Hey, sweetie," I called from the porch step, "I think the shoveling can wait until tomorrow."

At a community poetry reading on Saturday, John surprised me by fishing a folded *New York Times Book Review* from his coat pocket. As John's illness progresses and he requires constant support and supervision, he's still capable of the occasional reminder of who he was and of who he is. During the event held at our local bookstore, he leaned toward me and whispered in moments when he recognized friends and acquaintances, familiar faces minus names. He listened closely as readers took their turns at the podium. In other moments, he annotated the *Times* with a located pen. Scribbled words appeared in the margins of newsprint. Squiggles nestled under phrases and sentences. And for a few hours on a Saturday afternoon, John and I were an ordinary couple again, sustained by community and verse.

Estelle Bajou
DESPACITO

The box is longer than I am tall and half as heavy.
I circle it with arms, hug it to my right side like a giant baguette,
Let the door slam behind me.

Before reaching the third floor I'm sweating in my winter coat.
By the bottom step we rest, panting.
I wonder if it will find a good home.

An unattended ambulance blocks the driver from meeting me out front,
So I squeeze between parked cars and lumber down the street to meet
Him.

He rushes up, taking the box from my arms like I'm an old lady
Having an asthma attack.
Our facemasks billow a little as we smile our greetings.
I stand by the car with one eye on a flutter of sparrows
Dust bathing near a drain grate
While he tucks the instrument upright into the backseat
Like an oversized infant.

Buckled in, I admire his interior,
The shining black plastic,
Thoughtfully draped phone charger,
Poland Spring tucked into the seat pocket.

I admire his thin right arm draped across the passenger seat
As he looks past me, driving backward to Broadway.
I get a good look at the way his diaphanous lashes sweep
His forceful, black brows,
At his indulgent curls,
His showy gold watch.

I admire his cinnamon skin,
The deferential volume of Despacito playing on the radio,
His mindful blinkering between lanes.

If I'd had that baby in 2003, I'd have a child
Nearly his age.
Afternoon light blinks in memoriam
Against the stinging blue Hudson.

I send my thanks to his parents
Into the November air ruffling through the cracked windows,
Wonder how they managed.

When he deposits me and my piano on the sidewalk
In front of the pawn shop,
I see he knows I'm sending it away
And hope he understands it's only a question
Of endurance.

I send my wish to mingle with his mantle of Old Spice
That someone will love his sinewy nape,
His broad hands,
His keen, black eyes,

That he will find himself thunderstruck
Before an expanse of sea,
Or a couloir of red rock,
Or under a screen of leaves,
Or embosomed by fog,
At least once in his life,

That he will forgive me
As he drives away.

Alison Swan
IN THE EARLY DAYS OF IT

we constellated the yard,
>   stars that could still shoot —
backward into the street,
>   around the other side of the car.

Any shouted word could have carried it

so we air hugged and blew kisses,
>   circled one another
apart then closer then apart again —
>   not like wolves or dogs, though

sometimes together we formed their outlines —
>   no, we circled and wove
like wounded humans who,
>   having entirely lost their way,

still could not say to ourselves or to one another:
>   Open space succors.
True devotion crosses gaps easily.
>   Windtossed, sunlit,

we can emit devotion 24/7/365 without any risk at all.

Finally I had to close myself in and drive away.
>   We raced for miles,
my car and my heart. Here a street.
>   There a warehouse.

There a vast lot for storing cars alongside.
>   True night,

what's left of it, forming a kind of seawall.

Sprawl stacking up and up and up,
>   then at intervals, toppling,

carrying a zillion bits of the artificial light we crave.

Christine Pennylegion
PANDEMIC RESTRICTIONS, DAY 402

When a friend comes to visit you illegally
she comes to the back door, not the front.
There is a cake to celebrate reunion but
you're nervous the neighbours might see.

She comes to the back door, not the front,
bringing gifts of books and company.
You're nervous the neighbours might see
that. This visit has brought so much relief.

Bringing gifts: of books, and company
you didn't know how much you missed 'til now
that this visit has brought so much relief
you cry. A little after, she leaves.

You didn't know how much you missed, 'til now.
There is a cake to celebrate reunion, but
you cry a little after she leaves,
when a friend comes to visit you illegally.

Kelly Talbot
SEASON OF STEEL

A doe cries under an oak tree.
I do not understand.
I do not understand,
but I make a fist.
A hawk dives.
A carp dives.
An iron leaf, rusted, plummets past
a doe's eyes.
Under an oak tree, I am but a man.
The sky water dies hard.
Its corpses dive hard
to land, soft and crisp.
Ursa sleeps.
Brown blade sleeps.
The horizon melts into steel sheets.
Under an oak tree, a doe dies.
A man cries.
I understand.

Emma Karnes
PETTIBONE BEACH, LA CROSSE, WISCONSIN

So to go on loving, one must give up
the blue long tongue of the Mississippi.
Do I deserve to love, or to wiggle my body
through the cool gels of the enviable earth?
I lie, I curve, I toast on the edge
where the sun changes form.
I'm there, too, metamorphosing with June.
Whether I'm alone or an object
oozing among others, drowned or abreast,
silly for sitting here worshipping a pen,
or pretty strutting the beach with a beer,
the suspicions of the skeptics remain.
We all come to the shores of the river with pain.
We find it flows over us briefer than change.

Merritt Golick
RAINY SEASON

Last rainy season,
you held me when my clothes got moldy.
The days slogged on, a watercolor blur
of soaked-through shoes and sweat.

In a bed like a boat, on a steamy sea
we stewed. The rain fell, fell. I cried
and cried. Our broken umbrellas
piled up at the door.

This rainy season:
I'm dry as dust,

A universe away.

Holly Wren Spaulding
ESTUARY WALK

after Joy Harjo

A pink hairbrush is caught in the grass.
A single shoe and water bottle.
When the tide comes, all will
wash away—but where will it go?
A kingfisher calls—how did I
not know this sound until now?

We walk along the edge
before the sea fills in.
Pitch pine, scrub oak, juniper.
We admire the curves of this place—
Nauset land—where are they now?

My raincoat is torn, I'm never warm
in this season of wind
that wakes me up at night.
We circle toward home
as saltwater covers everything.

We touch hands, then make a photo
of ourselves as the sun
falls into the bay.
You look beautiful, you say.
Everything does
just before dark.

Katie Hartsock
BIRCHCREST AVENUE

I was so bored, I killed enough flies to spell my name.
—Elaine Stritch, on being sent outside
to play during summer vacation

See her take a final aim to dot the *i.*
A conjured portent of Broadway marquees.
Girl on a slab of well-heeled Detroit cement.
Her monument a wind could sweep away.
In that awful part of the afternoon
that gets her feeling like nothing.
So look what this laughing girl can do.
Wiping her hand on her romper
when the paper-flaky corpses are arranged,
as prophets must wipe their hands,
look what her sadness can make.
Such a spectacle that anyone
walking by speaks her name to the aether
as they read it on the ground.
Elaine? What?
A question spell.
She has tricked the world into casting it.
A choral incantation to end this day.
To never invite one like it into the yard again.
To send a telegram to the rest of her life.
To come take her away. Come now.
Come any minute now.

Kathleen Tighe
BIRDS OVER ARABIA

The morning cable show hosts argue over the latest dispatches from the Middle East: Are the troops coming home? Should any remain? Are we fighting ISIS or guarding oil? Caffeine fuels their discourse, each shouting over the other to gain more screen time.

I turn from the countertop TV and carry my mug to look out the window at the lake. The early morning sky reveals silver clouds hanging low, just above the steel grey waters of Lake Huron. A small flock of Canada geese skims the surface as they glide past, preparing for their annual migration south. Their clamorous calls fill the air, temporarily drowning out the contentious debate streaming from the TV. I watch until the birds are a thin thread on the horizon, just above the waterline. As I sip coffee, another image emerges unbidden from the sands of nearly 30 years of memory, and I am back in Saudi Arabia.

On that distant morning long ago, a similar darkness materialized on the horizon, contrasting with the dawn's pastel colors blending sea into sky. I stared as it grew larger, and soon I could discern moving shapes: birds, huge numbers of birds, flew across the Gulf, making their way toward the Arabian shore. I pointed it out to my husband, and Dan and I watched the birds cross the sky, just above the water's surface, and then overhead, flying silently and in utterly perfect formation, heading north. The flock soon faded, but as I swiveled back, I saw another line emerge out of the south, and then another. Hundreds, no, thousands of birds were migrating north, abandoning Africa and crossing the Arabian peninsula, making their long trek toward cooler summer climes.

The dark flocks spread across a vast open sky, their flight urgent against the sleepy morning as desert moved from its cool dark night into what soon would be blazing light. April in the desert was already high summer, and we would have broken camp and headed back to Khobar long before the sun hit noon.

We were not bird watchers, so we could not identify the birds. Parrots moved through the Eastern Province periodically; on the campus of the international school where I taught I sometimes spied their colorful feathers among the trees cultivated to provide scant shade in the blistering heat. We also spotted flamingos dotting the water's edge along the coast as we crossed the Bahrain Causeway for a weekend getaway from the harsh social restrictions of Saudi Arabia. These birds were neither.

"How many are there, do you think?" I asked.

"Hmm. Tens of thousands," Dan answered. "Look, they're still coming." He pointed toward the hazy pink horizon, the southern coastline too far to be seen from this shore. Thin black threads still surged from the distance.

One cool morning the previous January I stood, awestruck, as F-15s overtook the sky. Their shadows stretched across the tennis court where my friends and I played doubles, heading to the northern horizon. The engines' roar drowned the banter of partners as the game continued. Across the net, back and forth, the tennis ball flew. And across the sky, endlessly it seemed, the planes flew, white streams trailing in their wake, and I remembered the homesick pilots for whom I had cooked lasagne and apple pie the previous weekend. They shared stories of the war in exchange for an evening that felt a little like home, as this strange desert kingdom settled into darkness on the other side of my front door.

It was a quick war. By spring, the bombing raids on Kuwait had ended, and the black clouds spewing from burning oil wells left in the wake of Saddam Hussein's retreating troops had finally cleared. These birds we were watching now would fly over damaged oil rigs, oil-slicked beaches, exploded bridges, dead camels, and abandoned villages. They would pass over miles of ancient desert, just as others had every spring and fall, for thousands of years.

Today, from the comfort of my warm kitchen on a chilly autumn morning in Michigan, I gaze at the cold lake, envisioning the ice that will soon form, and the stillness it will bring. I think of those birds still migrating across the Gulf, that vast desert, the pools of oil waiting, deep and dark beneath it all.

Sherrill Alesiak
7335 HAMBURG
DETROIT 5, MICHIGAN

Perhaps to distract an eight-year-old,
my parents passed me Milky Ways
as the black-and-white movie, *Baby Doll,* crawled along.

Saturday evenings, my dad gaped at the X-rated film
playing at The Guild, just blocks away.
Going home, he'd stop at Alinosi's to bring us malts.

My mom shopped at Great Scott, washed floors on her knees.
My dad worked at the Chevy plant, shoveled snow, built a swing.
As our neighbors, we walked to church, donated clothing, bought a dog.

In spring, the petals of the magnolia in our yard
with but a touch, fluttered over the mowed lawn

Michelle DeRose
AUTUMN SESTINA

for Susan

Nothing heals without pain.
It's the same ritual every fall:
we move to the road the week's leaves.
A splayed hand with excess fingers,
the rake scrapes in the grass lines
that lead to curbside mounds.

As the colorful piles mount,
our lower backs twinge with pain
we address with scratched red lines.
The neighbor's children shriek and fall,
hurl to the sky with fat fingers
confetti swirls of heaved leaves.

At what point is childhood left
behind? When did our aches surmount
our mother's caress with gentle fingers,
her hugs, no longer anodyne for pains
and her arms, too weak to stop our falls?
When did deeper worries trace lines?

Life does not move in the measured lines
of middle school history. Our leave-
takings can surprise. Some born in spring die next fall.
So grief may mount.
The question's when, not if, with pain
and some knots can't be eased with fingers.

Practice in your hair: rake your fingers
along your scalp deeply enough for lines.
The tingle between relief and pain
is unpredictable: it comes and leaves.
The cat purrs and claws at the fur, mounding
off the comb as it falls.

So crimson maples tremble, detach, then fall.
We might twirl them between our fingers,
then toss them on the growing mounds.
We learn to color within the lines
we can bear, knowing that some leavings
surpass our threshold for pain.

In every curbside dome of leaves is the first that fell.
Our own fingers must manage the lines
that push them through pain to soft mounds.

Maggie Walcott
AGAINST THE GRAIN

The dog's fur was black and dense, each shaft fading from deep ebony to soft white the closer it got to the skin. Sarah stroked the fur one way and then the other, watching the patches of hair shift color. She remembered her father called this type of petting "going against the grain," as though it were something difficult to do. Unpleasant for the dog perhaps, but she had never met a dog that seemed to mind it. This dog sat patiently at her feet, waiting for a discarded toast edge or a fragment of uneaten bacon, as she ruffled its coat. Paul had finished his breakfast already and she kept her palm on the hound's soft coat as she cleared her throat softly to get his attention.

"Do you ever wonder whether dogs have souls?"

Paul put down his phone to peer up at her. He hadn't yet put his contacts in for the day and was still wearing his glasses, which she rather liked because it made him look like a slightly nerdier version of Clark Kent. Dr. Grassley had encouraged Sarah to find pleasure in the small things. This was one.

"I'm sure they do," he replied evenly. "I mean, they have personalities. Isn't personality just a reflection of the soul?"

Sarah shifted her hips in her chair. "No, not like that. Have you ever considered whether a *human* soul can be in a dog? Like, through reincarnation."

"Not really," he said, his voice coming slowly. She had surprised him, she thought. He had to let the words marinate for a moment in his mind before he could make sense of them. She pressed forward.

"Not really, like you don't think about it, or you don't think it's possible?"

"Not really, like I haven't ever thought about it," Paul replied.

"Well, do you? Do you think it's possible?"

"I don't know—maybe…" Paul's voice paused for a moment, considering. "What was it that Einstein said? Something like 'energy can be neither created nor destroyed.' So you know, maybe that energy has to go somewhere when we die. Then again, Einstein didn't believe in the afterlife, so," Paul's shoulders lifted slightly at that last and he glanced down furtively at his phone, before settling on his coffee cup instead.

Sarah had always appreciated this about Paul. Another small pleasure. The man had no sense of humor to speak of, never had, but you could ask him the most ridiculous questions and he would give you a generally thoughtful and serious answer. It had carried them through the long car rides to and from the hospital through the years.

Sarah looked down at the small dog at her feet, who had now given up on scrounging for scraps and was resting its nose on inky paws. The puppy was another suggestion from Dr. Grassley. Small pleasure number three. Or perhaps it had been Paul's suggestion, but echoed by Dr. Grassley. She couldn't recall anymore. Considering this, she was quiet just long enough for Paul to slide the black device off the table and back into his hand.

"It's just that, sometimes, I think that I see her in Lady."

A slight involuntary huff escaped Paul's lips. She could tell from the insight of years of spousal familiarity that Paul had already shifted gears. Had been ready, in fact, to move on entirely from this conversation. Then again, Paul was ever the perfect gentleman. Even when she desperately longed to see even the tiniest break in his control. She watched as he again placed the phone flat on the table and raised his eyes for one brief moment to look at Sarah directly. "See who in Lady?"

"Madeline."

At this, Paul's face pinched slightly, his eyes casting down to the table, as though to search for meaning in the misshapen oval whorls of the oak table. Meaning, or maybe forgiveness? Sarah had visited Madeline's grave on her own the day before. Perhaps conjuring their daughter's name was enough for Paul to regret his choice to stay behind. It had only been a year, for God's sake.

She continued before he could reply, "I know that sounds crazy, Paul. I know it does. But you know how Madeline was obsessed with that stuffed pig your sister sent her?" Paul nodded, his gaze still averted. Madeline had brought that pig everywhere with her: the grocery store, the library, doctors' offices, hospital rooms. The only reason they hadn't buried her with it was because Sarah couldn't bear to part with something her daughter had loved so well.

"Well yesterday, I found Lady lying with it in her dog bed. She must have gone into Madeline's room and grabbed it."

Clearing his throat, Paul replied, "Well, she is still technically a puppy, Sarah. She likes toys. You know that. I'm sure one of us left the door open and she just took the opportunity to grab a stuffed animal." Paul's hand reached for the mug of coffee on his right, still warm but fading fast.

"You haven't been in that room in two months. We both know that. And *I* didn't leave the door open," Sarah continued. "It was just that one animal, Paul. She could have grabbed any of them lying on Madeline's bed, but she didn't. She chose that one. She left the others untouched and brought that toy specifically to her kennel, where she's had it for God knows how long and hasn't destroyed it. You know how careful Madeline was with that toy."

Sarah waited as Paul's hands clasped together around his coffee cup, a nervous tic he was unaware of, each finger laddered on top of its opposing hand mate, thumbs looped safely in the handle of the mug, lightly brushing against each other for comfort. *Up, up and away we go*, Sarah thought.

"I don't think that's a healthy thought process, Sarah. Remember what Dr. Grassley said? He told us that if we want to make progress, we have to let go of the what-ifs."

Sarah noticed Paul had employed the royal *we*, when in fact they both knew perfectly well who struggled with progress. Always so considerate, her husband. *We* left the door open. *We* have to attend therapy twice a month. *We* have to let go. She had always appreciated his consideration in the past, but lately it had begun feeling different. Unintentionally condescending. Meant to be soothing, but instead abrasive. Against the grain.

Unexpected anger rippled through her core and spread to her face, her forehead suddenly feverishly hot. She didn't need him to pretend that they grieved in the same way. She knew better. Hell, he couldn't even look her in the eye most days; ashamed of her, ashamed of himself—she didn't know.

Even now, Paul's gaze rested on Lady's face. A mistake. He hadn't watched the change in his wife as her facial muscles morphed from cautious optimism to defensive guard to unchecked fury. He went unwittingly ahead: "Have you thought about making an appointment with Dr. Grassley again?"

Wrapping her hands around the edge of the table, Sarah felt the anger erupt from her body, tangible and raw. "Fuck Dr. Grassley, Paul! And fuck you, too—you're not the one going to her grave every week. You're not the one in there cleaning her room, or taking tiny pills to sleep at night. What I need is for you to stop telling me what I need. I'm already doing it. You're not. She's not gone, Paul. I know it. I'm certain of it."

The dog, startled by the sudden uproar, emerged from underneath the table where no more scraps were forthcoming anyway, and plodded toward the safety of her kennel. Watching it leave, Sarah was surprised to find her words coming faster now.

"See what you've done, Paul? You've upset her. Jesus, why do I have to do all the work? Always me. Me, convincing you. JUST DO SOMETHING ALREADY, PAUL." The final words were spat out, bitter spray forced through clenched teeth, while hot tears followed the curve of Sarah's reddened cheeks before settling in the folds of her neck. The wood under Sarah's hands felt cool to the touch — soothing. She used that leverage to push up, to move away from the table and shuffled quickly out of the room.

Paul, alone once more, unclasped his fingers from the death grip they had formed around the coffee mug, and opened them wide to receive the weight of his head. One thumb on each side of his jaw, the other fingers peppered lightly across his forehead, his hooded eyes trailed the path his wife had taken. *Surely*, he thought, *this is something.*

Michael Hughes
IN HER OWN TIME

Don't worry Dad, I'll be fine.
New life sprouting inside,
she is tense and athletic
as she grips his arm
and smiles their way to the altar.

She arranged the wedding in a week.
He paid the bills.
Who gives this woman?
He offers her hand
sits down on a rigid bench.

After, he wanders among strangers.
Guests relax their concentration.
Many leave before gifts are opened,
two small boxes and a pile of cards.

Someone photographs his daughter
running out with her man
a small group blowing bubbles
and again as she drives off in a silver Mustang
cans clanking, windows written in white
Scandalous No Mo'.

This was not his dream for her.

He sees himself in her eyes, mouth, chin,
the stubborn, tight jaw even as a child,
and smiles for the first time today.

She is short-sighted but speaks a young truth –
will take every back road
bounce over the deepest ruts
and still make it home
in her own time
just fine.

Roy Bentley
IMAGINING MYSELF MY MOTHER

after Stephen Dunn

Tonight, I'm a woman dancing with the wrong man in the
wrong room in Flint Ridge Nursing Home in Newark, Ohio —

I'm seventy-nine and wearing the Harley jacket my adult son
drapes over my scarecrow-thin shoulders to slow shenanigans.

If I'm virtually a ghost, I'm also flesh-connected. I used to run
up and down the high-school basketball court in Fleming-Neon

and in the other coal towns. I used to sweat like a spigot opened.
Even in picnic weather, brilliant blue sky cheering the dispirited.

Listen. If I am the Freewill Baptist church, I'm also that tavern
where two of my brothers were murdered over next to nothing.

I stand to instruct a son in the fine art of shooting free-throws.
Good coaching teaches the basketball star to keep best moves

for late in the game. Undeniably, for me, it's late in the game.
I remember her saying *You miss all the shots you don't take.*

Ellen Stone
HOUNDSTOOTH JACKET

They say the pattern is like teeth
but all you see are birds like pheasants
in the hedge, or geese lined up there —
whole rows of them, soldiers in the sky
above the field. Jumble in the fall before
the woods become all golden. Gathering
they take off in legion shapes that fill
the clouded blue with darkened points.
The wool is green of lichen-under-pine
and in the sun, a little thread of hidden
rust or almost red of winterberry.
Buttons — some knobs of orange seeped
into brown, wood mushrooms that show
up near a rotting log just after rain.

Its boxy jacket shape, the way an old
school room was square with desks
of oaken frame lined up. It needs a pipe
and even then, a dog, the hunter-type
that lies down near the feet to keep
them warm and only comes when called
or when it's time to put the coat back
on, pack up the coffee thermos, head
out into the rest of day, the scratchy
collar pulled up around his neck. Now
the moths have found their way into
the sleeves and back, and you can see
through tiny holes, as if a peek-a-boo.
But you remember how it felt against
your skin, a whiskered itch and scratch
the musky leathered smell of hounds.

Jennifer Fandel
FISHING WITH MY FATHER

He would not have used the word *unequivocal*
to describe the sky, one cloud parsing itself
into a heart, old and beating, dark gray bottom
filled with storm. That's my word

for a day of flannel and wool, our boat
drifting with the riffles the wind made
on the lake, our casts fast against the chill
in our bones. He approached his task

as if he were young again, impatiently
patient for the lurch of the muskellunge,
a fish so tough to catch that a snag felt
as close to death as birth.

He did not speak. I did not speak.
Here was a man turning toward sunset,
and I could only imagine this tough
and beautiful world going down with him.

Sara Dudo
DIMMING

There was a time Dad was at the glass-sliding door
shooting groundhogs with his .22; I watched
through the bathroom blinds as the bullet hit.

Growing old is deciding not to retrieve the gun
from the cellar these days, letting them comb his ground.

I ask him to consider the life of the traffic light on Tuckahoe,
how many times we've passed it by and if it notices

any striking resemblance in our Irish eyes, open mouths
singing to a hand-me-down radio, left arm farmers tan.

There was a night the power went out and we played
Kings in the Corner in lantern-light of a tornado warning,
not wanting to be buried in sleep. In her bed, my mother
tossed her body onto exchanging hips.

It'll save the electric bill, he concurs, and I consider
how much energy goes into keeping a room lit, how
to make the most of it.

Now, we squish mulberries laying on the pavement
every time summer pulls itself over the crest of spring.
Neighbors with glistening brows spray for tomato worms,

and I trust no one, I watch the rusting wheel circulate under
my father's body, waiting for stone to pop or chain
to catch. I wait for disaster hidden in the sunlight rolling
like a breaker across the street, hidden in him, in me.

Growing old is a choice between a lack of trust in anything
when you feel most at home, and getting over it.
And, lately, my father is the safest room in the house.

Natalie Welber
THE BASEMENT

after Marie Howe

Praise to this prowling cricket, monstrous
through no fault of its own, twitching its pincers across

the desert expanse of rust red carpet. An earthy alien on Mars, it does not belong
indoors. I pray it stays far away, too wary of the exotic wood and nails

to scale the mountain of bed before it. This bed
my grandmother died in, now my haven safe above the ground where I hide

from the sound that even now leaches through the house. The breathing machine
churning an ocean to pure oxygen, tempest loud to me, must be

the sound of galaxies colliding, all inhabitants dying,
to the tiny bug.

The alien stalks slowly, like the grotesque necropolis of its former family,
earlier astronauts now crucified in sticky, tricky glue. This cricket

has learned from its forebears' fates to avoid the trap. It lifts a leg, steady, ready
to catch its prey upon the bed, which creaks as I cower away, like the bones

that once gave out upon it. The bed of the woman who died, whose daughter
is dying upstairs right now. Any minute until the oxygen tides recede.

Any moment until the alien reaches me. I don't know
if I can bear to crush it, to touch it, to even flick it away.

Praise the cricket. Praise it.
It is so simple to be afraid of this.

Ron Riekki
(50) MY BODY IS BEAT TO HELL

but don't tell Hell. Or Heaven. Or any of the dead
yet. Six years to live, from what I've read online.
Which is two thousand poems, if I do one a day. One
liver cyst that's idiopathic, meaning it leaves doctors
feeling like they're on the pathway of idiots, shrugging
shoulders, scratching heads, no idea. And suicidal
ideation, under control, thank God, understood, sort of,
from countless counseling where they make me count
breaths, slowly, in and out, exhale till you feel exhale-ent,
she says, and she's right, breath is a good thing—death

and breath so flirtatious with each other. And my body
flirts with hurt constantly, chronically, how pain is so
good at owning the world when it wants to. My back
taken, ironically, by hauling patients with bad backs,
EMT days, or, more correctly, EMT nights, where you
get a dollar extra for midnight shift, that dollar to help
you get through the ghosts of the basements of hospitals
we'd frequent, the patients with such an infinity of
deformities, contusions, abrasions, punctures and
penetrations, burns, tenderness, lacerations, swelling,

and orchestras of yelling. And now I yell, last night—
swear to God—getting stitches with no anesthetic,
how you fall more with age, how you age more with
falls, how the autumn is leaving, winter coming for-
ever. And my head, yes, my head, God, my head,
where I want to warn everyone out there to limit
your concussions, that they add up exponentially,
the doc saying my tremors are linked to traumas,
the nurse saying my tremors are linked to memories,
the medic saying my tremors are merely just tremors,

that he's more worried about bleeding, paralysis,
altered mental status, that a vibrating body is nothing.
And I think of my body being nothing. And I put my
head back on the gurney, looking up at the ceiling
that has been coughed on a few thousand times and
never been washed. And we get to the E.R. and we
get to the trauma center and we get to the psych ward
and we get to the clinic and I realize that, in my mind,
it's a dream, where sometimes I'm the medic, some-
times I'm the EMT, and sometimes I'm the patient,

and sometimes I'm me, all three. My body helping
bodies, and then my body needing help. And the one
thing I learned while working in health was that
there's nothing tougher on the body than working
in health. And it's too late to know this, like when
I delivered pizzas for one summer where at the end
all those miles put on my car had it run down and
the shop calculated how much it would cost to fix it
and it was exactly as much as all of the money I'd made
because, my God, there is nothing weirder than God.

Anthony Otten
THE RED MASS

On election day Judge Trippi won a full term for the family court
seat in our county. Her opponent was a fundamentalist Mormon
with an online law degree and a spare wife he couldn't keep in his
basement. It wasn't close; so we figured our jobs were safe.
Judge's alma mater, St. Francis College, offered her the keynote
following the annual Red Mass for their alumni in the legal
profession. Judge was very Catholic: she prayed the rosary with
her left hand in the car while steering with the right. And it was
her dream—somewhat childishly, she admitted, for a woman of
forty-three—to give that speech before the senile old relics who had
taught her during undergrad.

A month into her new term, the Judicial Conduct
Commission slapped a dozen accusations on Judge's desk in a fat
FedEx mailer. St. Francis withdrew the keynote. They handed
it to our office neighbor and nemesis, Judge Flake—His Honor
Dandruff, we called him out of earshot.

When I entered Judge's office the next morning, she had
already poured a glass from the bottle in her desk.

"No judge," she said after the second drink, "has ever been
treated so unfairly. Nobody would argue that."

"Is it because you're the first Hispanic lady elected in the
county?"

"Not quite. I'm not as Mexican as you'd think."

"You were at the Hispanic Chamber for the—"

"People assume. You let them assume, if it helps," she said.
"I might have some Italian on my grandma's side."

"Well, I'm sorry."

"Why don't you like Italians?"

"I meant for the charges."

"Frick that, Gail. It's the keynote that kills me. Charges are
one thing, but losing your engagements? That's how Alicia Trippi
becomes yesterday's big laugh."

"They could invite you next year after you're cleared," I
said.

"They won't get the chance. St. Francis is closing."

"Why's that?"

"I can guess. The place costs sixty grand a year and the hot water doesn't work."

"It had to be good at some point," I said. "You went there."

Judge let me have a smile. She got up and nudged the door shut with one stiletto. In the sky framed by her eighth-floor windows, a news helicopter, wasp-sized, zipped over the rooftops. I dropped my pen as she leaned into my view. Her mouth tasted like Fireball and peach lipstick.

I said, "Hank's next door. He'll be jealous."

"Yes, he will," she said.

Hank was Judge's case manager. Before that, he had been the music director at her church. He and I tried to keep our hormones out of the office. Judge didn't need two of her staff clashing like kids at a prom while she was weighing divorces, custody fights, alimony — more broken families than you could fit in a Walmart. The rivalry still thrilled me, though. It was just too unlikely a thing for somebody like Gail Somerset — a wannabe librarian in bifocals with a twenty-two year marriage behind her. A lady who liked her cat more than her cat liked her.

I met the courthouse crew about a year after Bob left and the twins went to college. Judge knew me from the funeral committee at St. Barbara's. She heard I was alone most nights and asked me over to watch her band practice. I was the only invite; the attorneys had to be there. They practiced in her courtroom and called her Alicia outside it, at her insistence. In her basement they lounged on the vinyl couches or held up their phones to the ground-level windows, fishing for a signal. They were all educated, and really sour, but not just to me. So I thought it was kind of funny. Judge's band was called Rearview Mirror and mostly did '70s and '80s covers. Journey, Aerosmith, that stuff. Judge gave me a CD. I think she always liked me better than Hank. He was the front man on the bass guitar, tall and kidney-headed, gingery sideburns like the red panda hanging from a tree at the zoo. I don't know what made her want him. He was a Charismatic — maybe he spoke in tongues. Judge liked to collect exotic things.

Judge handed me a tambourine. "Here, come up and beat on that. Just keep the tempo."

We rattled the whole block. I could imagine the neighbors calling the non-emergency dispatch as Judge bellowed into the mic. The attorneys either sank into their emails or stared at us like they were waiting for the negotiators to arrive. I loved it. I felt the sort of freedom I only had when I was asleep. I wasn't dwelling on the meaning of Bob's sporadic texts, wasn't worrying how fast Dylan was driving or Alexis was going with the new guy. I felt like Gail wasn't even there.

During a break one of the attorneys asked Judge if he could duck out. He had a crew cut and a Navy tattoo on his neck.

"You've got the Manning divorce on Tuesday?" she asked.

"Yes, ma'am."

"All right," she said. "Good luck with that."

Everybody watched as he froze, slouched back in the recliner, and took out his phone again. Hank and I grinned behind Judge's back. She was like Hillary Clinton. Kind of mean, but you loved her.

"Performance at The Bayou on Saturday, kids," she told the attorneys when they were dismissed. "If you haven't volunteered to come, you have now been volun-told."

The drummer and the keyboardist packed their instruments. Hank had a surly look and kept slurping his Diet Pepsi with a suddenness that made me wince. I guess after everybody left it was supposed to be his playtime with Judge, even though her kids were upstairs watching TV; she had them on weekends. He got madder when she only shared the pot with me.

"Weed has estrogen in it," she told him. "It shrinks a man down there."

"Well, don't smoke too much or you'll have Ellen DeGeneres at the door," he said.

"I love Ellen," she said.

We listened to him stomping out to his wife's Tahoe, the engine shuddering awake.

"He doesn't like girls that like girls," Judge said. "But I like everybody."

"His loss."

"My secretary just quit," Judge said. "You looking for work?"

"I'm a teacher's aide."

"Perfect," she said. "I manage these attorneys just like kids. Who gets to talk and when they get to talk. Bathroom breaks. Lunch. We even have recess around noon."

I was laughing.

"You sound rusty, Gail. You haven't laughed in a long time, have you?"

"There's a lot I haven't done in a long time," I said.

We were in the downstairs bathroom for a while and then we talked about the job.

"Hank needs work too," she said. "The church cut him to part-time. I think I'll make him case manager. I have to get rid of that lady doing it now."

Just for my first week, Judge let me use her secure elevator that went straight from the parking garage to the eighth floor. Hank caught me coming out one day. When he saw it was me, his smile dropped faster than his pants ever had.

After the Conduct Commission filed those charges, however, Hank and I agreed to a truce for Judge's sanity. Reporters were camping at the courthouse door like a horde of gnats. The office echoed with their phone calls.

When I was in the break room washing out Judge's mug I heard Judge Flake in his chambers with Missy, his assistant.

"Strippy Trippi," Flake said.

Missy laughed. "Stop it. You can't be —"

"I can't get tripped up on this."

Missy threw in: "You're tripping over Trippi."

"It's her fault. She's on quite the trip."

They howled. I imagined Missy sitting on Flake's lap, polishing his half bald head. I banged the mug in the sink.

"I'm gonna steal his Life Alert," I said in Hank's office.

Hank shrugged. He was practicing riffs on his guitar. "If he's throwing mud at Alicia, maybe we could throw worse mud at him."

"Like how?"

"Like go to the news. Say he creeps on you at work."

"Nobody would care."

"Say he pinned you against the wall. Arm around your throat."

"An old man?"

"You haven't seen what old folks can do. My aunt's in a home. She knocked out a nurse with her cane. A male nurse."

I could see he was playing, that it was academic to him. Like anybody who's married, he only really cared about the people he had to live with. He had a whole elementary school PTA of hussies to choose from if his thing with the Judge fizzled. But I grabbed at his idea.

"You and me. In his chambers. When they're out for lunch. Loudly."

"Are we playing Clue?"

"I'm serious."

"I don't hit just anything."

"I don't mean really doing it. Just faking it. When the cleaning lady comes in."

"She's supposed to spread the rumor?"

"Everybody talks," I said.

"What if she calls the bailiff? Or animal control?"

I ignored that. "My ex and I did it once, to freak out my in-laws. We were next door to their bedroom on vacation."

"You ever do it with him for real?"

"Come on, Hank. This lady gave you a job, and you won't help her? I'd hate to get a flat tire and only have you in my phone."

So we waited for Flake and Missy to leave. When the cleaning lady rolled her trash cart down the hall, we darted into Flake's office and locked ourselves in. We leaned our ears at the door until we heard the lady spritzing Windex. Sitting cross-legged on the rug, I rocked and groaned with a gusto that Bob had never heard. Hank lifted a chair and steadily thudded it on the wall.

"Marvin, oh Marvin," I said.

"Is that his name?"

"Yes," I hissed: "Marvin, oh God."

"Missy."

"Yes."

"Missy."

"Yes," I said, and a knock thundered on the door. We stopped. The cleaning lady spewed an impatient breath.

"Got to come back later," she muttered. "Rude."

The cart wheeled out of Flake's suite.

"She must be deaf as shit," Hank said.

We fled back to his office, too spooked for another attempt, and marinated our failure with a couple Bud Lights from his mini fridge.

After a while he said, bemused, "You know, you could have her. She seems to mean a lot to you."

"I can't tell if you're kidding. I wouldn't take that deal."

"Why not?" His married smirk.

"Because then you'd be giving her to me. I want her to kick your ass to the curb."

He could laugh, when he drank. "Be careful how close you stick to Alicia. You'll end up in jail with her."

"They haven't charged her with a crime. Just technicalities."

"But you'd like it. Sharing a cell with her. Same bunk. You would."

"You have no class," I said, and slurped.

"Gail in jail. It even rhymes."

"You'll be getting a divorce before they ever lock me up," I said.

It was that week I found Judge bawling by her office window, mascara spidering from the corners of her eyes.

"Alicia, what in the world?"

"Hank quit," she cried. "He flipped. They flipped him on me."

"You know that for sure?"

"I know a fucking rat," she said. "God, I let him drive my car. His stink's going to be in it forever. I'd get a new one but I might not have a job soon."

I remembered Hank's offer to let me have Judge. It might not have been a joke; he would have wanted the distance between him and Judge if his wife heard about them.

"Did you call Ted?" I asked. That was her attorney.

"Yeah. I fired him," she said through a sniff. "He told me I should come clean and say they're overreacting. But you don't admit to these things. You fight. Somebody called me a mafia queen in that report."

"That's racist against Italians."

"You're damn right." She yanked the window cord. The blinds shot up in a roll.

"I'll jump, Gail. Swear to God. It's the quicker exit."

"Messy," I said, unperturbed. She had to know those windows didn't open.

"When has messy ever scared me off?" she said.

The second big cry happened in Judge's living room after the Conduct Commission heard Hank's testimony and voted, unanimously, to remove her from the bench. I handed Judge a Kleenex and my compact. "I would say call in a favor with the Governor, but..."

"Him? He couldn't even get *himself* reelected. What could he do for me? Wouldn't I be better off with a razor blade in the bathtub?"

"You'd miss the keynote. Isn't it Thursday?"

"I'm not invited."

"And you care?"

Judge looked back at me with a shrewd gleam. "You could be right. I'm not thinking like Trippi. I'm thinking like—"

"A loser."

She grinned to herself. Then: "You'll go with me?"

She sent me to Neiman Marcus with the office MasterCard, which she had kept, to hunt for an outfit. I picked out a bright red pantsuit. I shivered with my fingers on the polyester, knowing her body would be inside it. Inspired when I got home, I Googled Hank's wife—she was the preschool teacher at his church—and sent her an unsigned email:

ask hank where judge has a tattoo

That was it. He had spared me any mention in his testimony, but he should have known that crossing Judge was crossing me. If I was smart I would have texted him before he ever talked to the commission: *You want Carly to hear about Mickey Mouse?* I could have reeled him back from betrayal, saved Judge's job. But I was never good at being bad; I just had my fun.

On Thursday I picked up Judge in the Audi I'd bought with my half of Bob's checking account. She stunned me posing in front of her three-car garage—clothed in red, with black heels, like a prophetic vision of the whore of Babylon. Over her left breast she had pinned a big brooch. It was a crimson A.

"You look like you need a chauffeur," I said.

"I need a parade, is what I need."

"What's the A for?"

She looked disappointed: "Alicia, of course. They're not gonna forget it."

Judge made me stop at the 7-Eleven for a pack of cheese crackers to hold her through lunch. We were late for the Red Mass. We tiptoed into the last row, genuflecting and crossing ourselves. "You're okay as long as you make it by communion," Judge whispered. The two priests were dressed all in red like her. They reminded me of the monsters in that movie where everybody lives in an old village and can't leave. Bob liked that one.

When we checked in at the luncheon, the greeter offered to make her a name tag in Sharpie; she wasn't on the list. She patted the big A. "This'll be good enough."

A big brown-suited man stopped us before we went into the banquet hall. He had a childish face with gopher jowls, as if he had bought a new face to slap over the old one. "Alicia...I saw you in the back at church. I should've known you wouldn't stay there."

"Sorry if I'm late. I had to stop for confession."

"I'll bet you did." He smiled indulgently, but his eyes were hard gray pebbles. His name tag said he was head of the alumni association.

"This is Gail, my partner," Judge said. "In crime."

"This lunch is invitation only," the head told her. "You certainly aren't on the list."

"I'm here to give my talk, Randy. Not to argue."

"Judge Flake took your spot."

"Flake had some trouble this morning," Judge said. "He wants me to step in. You shouldn't be surprised. His name says it all."

The head warmed from pink to ruby. He pulled out his cell phone. "I'll get Judge on the line," and he stepped into the campus security office, following us with his stare. We went on into the banquet hall and sat at a front table with a centerpiece of roses and a little card that said *Reserved – Brian Finn, Esq. and Family.*

"What happened to Flake?" I asked.

"I drained his tank in the driveway. Like you do when there's a hurricane and the gas stations run out. All you need is a garden hose and some good suction."

A few minutes later the head came for us, swollen with offense. "Alicia, you're trespassing."

"Did you need a judge to give you that opinion?"

"If you don't leave, the law will have to get involved," he said.

"The law's already here," she said. "Me."

The cops bargained with Judge: they wouldn't cuff her and she wouldn't fight. I surrendered voluntarily too, and that was the first time anybody in the hall looked at Gail Somerset. They put Judge and me in the back of the same patrol car for the trip down to the precinct.

"You got your parade," I said.

"I wonder if they'll put us in the same cell?" she said.

"Not for long, they won't."

Bail wasn't that bad, but I had to spot Judge some cash. "Things are a little tight with me," she said. I regretted saying I had the money. It was like with Hank's wife, I just didn't think. Judge and I could have been the only friends we knew who had stayed a night in jail. We could have been together.

Robin Gow
EUPHEMISM

We went family planning all through the new year. Him, putting all
the dogs to sleep and me occupied with my female hygiene. I didn't
want to look at his collateral damage anymore so, I went on with
my negative cash flow. Everyone I love is between jobs. Everyone
I love is croaking. We powder our noses. We are over the hill and
picking up speed. His elevator doesn't reach the top floor and mine
is chronologically challenged. I turned one too many tricks and now
I'm just a street. Even the birds and the bees are afraid of us. We
don't even go all the way anymore—we just touch first base and
keep running. I'm okay with being a comfort woman but there's no
comfort and no woman. He opts for self-service in the garage. No one
I know is well-to-do but many are developing countries. I want to be
with child if it means we get to sleep together.

He is adult content. I am an adult content. Nothing is more graphic
than mornings. The gentlemen's club is now accepting couples like
us. I'm expecting. I'm expecting. We fell off the wagon so long ago
it's not worth even tracing the road home. Tell me about your friendly
fire and I'll tell you about mine. The bedroom requires the supreme
sacrifice from us all.

Cynthia Boorujy
THE COMMENTS SECTION

"Not to brag, but back in the day I roasted some gorgeous chickens," Lillian reported from behind her menu. Ken took in the scene around him. Although he was hesitant about choosing a new unproven restaurant, The Parsonage was firing on all cylinders. Big picture window, nicely spaced tables and William Morris wallpaper in the classic "Strawberry Thief" print. He had coveted the paper for his own dining room, but at $186.00 a roll he'd had to say "No, thank you." Each table had a polished brass candlestick holder with a beeswax taper: a possible fire hazard. But the long, thin candles gave off an air of a bygone time, of Charlotte Bronte writing into the night squinting from her growing myopia. Next to his plate he placed a small Moleskin notepad and pen. Today's journalists probably recorded interviews on their phones, but he preferred the old-world approach.

Ken wasn't sure how to respond to Lillian's statement. He didn't know if she was lamenting the fact that she would no longer be roasting chickens, or if she was playing a game of one-upmanship. He decided to steer the conversation in another direction and commented on how lovely the early evening light was streaming through the restaurant's front window. He hadn't been on the mainland in quite some time, and looking at it through a new frame felt both thrilling and disorienting.

Lillian lowered her menu. "Yes. They do a nice job of cleaning the glass here." Did she mean that as a compliment? Or was it sarcastic—as if clean windows were the least she expected of a restaurant. He looked at her for clues, but found none.

"I mentioned the chickens," Lillian said, "because they have it on the menu. *Roasted chicken with fingerling potatoes and maple-glazed Brussels sprouts.* I never order something in a restaurant that I can make easily and better at home."

"Fair enough," Ken responded. "No chicken for you." Lillian flipped the menu over and slid it away so it cantilevered over the edge of the table. Her posture erect and impeccable, she let her gaze settle on Ken. "What is your stand on Brussels sprouts?" she leveled at him.

"The maple glazing sounds nice. Could be a good counterpoint to the savory elements?" he floated, hoping it sounded erudite, only to see her raise her brows and purse her lips. "What do you think of them?" he added quickly.

"Devil's testicles. That's what I call them. Horrible stuff, no matter what you do to them. I wouldn't touch them if you paid me."

This wasn't at all how Ken envisioned her. The real-life version of Lillian was nothing like the helpful Grande Dame of the comments section he had come to admire and, admittedly, obsess over since he had subscribed to *The New York Times* cooking section a year ago. Ken was among five or six regulars, a sort of unofficial cooking club, who commented on each recipe and offered tips to novice cooks on how the recipe could be tweaked or improved. *LillianKnowsBest* initially caught his eye when she mentioned spotting roadside stands of pickled fiddleheads and mused that the sight of them always signified the start of spring to her. Knowing fiddleheads only grew in their area of the country, Ken formulated a sense of neighborly solidarity with her. His cooking crush was solidified the first time she commented on his comment and called it "Spot on!" Online, she never disappointed, repeatedly and reliably dispensing gem after gem.

In response to a seafood paella recipe, she recalled spending a summer traipsing around Spain with a girlfriend, setting up easels in shady doorways before she assured fellow readers there was no need to agonize about not having the right vessel: any large skillet would produce a redolent feast as long the home cook took care to add the ingredients in the proper order. A recipe for Buche de Noel elicited memories of her childhood. Within the word count allotted, she unspooled a story of her father and uncle driving through town at midnight in their 1963 Corvette and ringing sleigh bells for all the children awaiting Santa Claus before suggesting to add a bit of coffee liqueur to the batter and spraying the parchment as well as the pan.

"You're wincing," Lillian said. "Is it because I used the word *testicles*? Or that I combined it with the devil? You're a man of the cloth; do I have that right?"

"Oh, not cloth per se. I'm a knitter," Ken clarified.

"No, stupid. Religion. You never heard that expression: *man of the cloth*? I thought you said you were a pastor in your email. Did I get that wrong? It was rather verbose. I started to skim after the first paragraph."

"No, I never said that," Ken said, trying to keep his composure after being called stupid. She didn't mean it that way, he told himself. It was probably an expression people of her generation used, not thinking it would cause hurt feelings. The way his mother had called him stupid so he would strive to be better. Lillian gave a little snort and picked the menu up again.

Ken wasn't sure how to proceed. Maybe he should start asking some of his prepared questions, but it might be bad form to launch right in before they had even ordered their meals. Perhaps he should cut his losses and leave now. But the thought of disappointing Jonathan was too much.

Jonathan ran the yarn store where Ken bought his knitting supplies. He was also the editor of the local island newspaper. The last time Ken stopped in to stock up on heathered charcoal merino wool, Jonathan had mentioned he was looking to add some variety to the food column. "I'm a man down, though. Bryan used to do all the restaurant reviews but he can't do it any more with his colitis acting up. And I don't know if people can take any more of my sad little soup recipes." He said it nonchalantly as he totaled up the order, adding, "By the way, I saw you updated your Etsy store. I love your stuff. All your sweaters are so classy and refined. You should switch it up, though. Go wild. Maybe try some macramé. It might be fun!" He tossed a free ball of multi-colored hemp into the bag and topped it off with his million-dollar smile.

Ken beamed the whole walk home and as soon as he got in and fed his cats, he emailed Jonathan and floated the idea of interviewing a food expert. He fudged the truth a bit and said he had gotten to know a local woman who regularly published in *The New York Times*. It was sort of the truth. The comments were published. Online. Jonathan wrote back immediately, "*Great! You're awesome!!*"

Feeling inspired, Ken opened a bottle of pinot and decided to tackle a beef bourguignon (5-star rating). He thought of emailing Jonathan back and asking him to come around for dinner. Should he? Too bold? Well, better to get the dish started and see how it was going. As usual, he checked the comments section before starting. Hmmm. Some readers thought the oven temp was a bit high and short. Others said they had cooked as directed and it was delicious. He scanned for *LillianKnowsBest* to see her take. True to form, she eloquently expounded on the beauty of taking your time by bypassing the hour and half in the oven and instead cooking on the stove for 4-5 hours. She wrote that she had used the time to oil the wood on her rolltop desk while gazing out the window at gently falling leaves. She had included the phrase: "as I stared out at the intersection of Seaview and Bright Sky." While at first glance it had sounded merely poetic Ken realized it was indeed the mainland town of Firth Cove that she spoke of. He had always found it amusing that the town's founders had chosen such optimistic street names for a place that was overcast 85% of the year.

He did a quick satellite search on Google maps and then switched to street view. He copied down all the street addresses that would have a view of the intersection and looked up purchase history. Within seconds he found 1342 Bright Sky Road registered to a Lillian Snell.

By the time he had sleuthed out Lillian he had soured on the idea of asking Jonathan to come by. The meal wouldn't be ready until nearly midnight and what kind of message would that send? Jonathan was way out of Ken's league attractiveness-wise, and Ken had no intention of being overt about his feelings. Better to play his strong suit and remain aloof. What had Jonathan called his sweaters? Refined. Yes. He sat with that for a minute.

He did the next best thing and set to making the dinner chatting out loud as if Johnathan was there. "My cardigans have been selling well. I love when people appreciate a soft dove grey." He paused, imagining Jonathan's responses in his head. "Have another glass! I bought an extra bottle just in case." With the music going and the aromas filling the house it felt full and lively. He could hardly tell he was alone.

"I'm going with the filet mignon. Let's hope they know what rare means," Lillian huffed.

"Oh, I was planning on getting that," Ken said, feeling thrown off guard. "But I guess I'll go with the fish of the day. So, you know, we're not ordering the same thing." He reached into his pocket and fiddled with his lighter. He had stopped smoking years ago but never rid himself of the habit of carrying a lighter with him.

"Oh, Christ. What do you think we're going to do, hunch over our plates with our forks entwined and share our petite morsels? I hope you didn't think this was a date."

"No. Not at all. I just thought sometimes it's nice to taste more than one thing on the menu. Never mind." Ken could feel his face getting hot. *I hope you didn't think this was a date* dredging up memories of encounters he actually thought were dates. What was she thinking? She had to be in her sixties, old enough to be his mother. Maybe even seventies. She had a cane propped next to her chair. A grandmother! Not to mention the fact that he assumed everyone could tell he was gay.

"Shall we get this started?" she prompted. "I suppose you want to start with the basics. My influences. My philosophy on cooking. Or would you like me to lead you through how to do this?" Ken grasped the edge of the tablecloth with his fingers, trying to center himself by figuring out the fiber content.

"Yes, let's start with your influences."

"My grandmother was my influence. I know that sounds typical. You know, cooking with Grandma in the kitchen, passing down recipes from the homeland. Except it wasn't like that. I didn't have a little Italian grandma. She was a big tough Mainer through and through. All grey skies and darned socks. Never traveled anywhere, but collected cookbooks from all over the world. We created all sorts of things. It was always a challenge getting ingredients but that's how we learned to tweak things. Every time we'd try a recipe from a new country she'd give me a book to read that related to it, so I could learn something about that country. I think she felt some pressure to overdo it with me. My mother skipped out when I was a baby and I never knew dear old Dad."

"Wait. Really? What about that story you wrote about your dad and your uncle driving through town with the sleigh bells?"

"Oh that. You remembered that one? That was my neighbor. It sounded better to make it my father." Ken put down his pen and took a sip of his water.

"That doesn't sound like good practice."

"What?" Lillian shifted in her chair.

"Making things up in *The New York Times*. It's a newspaper of note."

"Relax. I know your type is finicky for details. Following rules and such, but no one is fact-checking the comments section."

Ken felt a twinge of pride at being considered in the same league as a real journalist. Not that he ever harbored aspirations of being a writer—he just liked the idea of being well respected. In charge of the narrative. He also liked the way journalists dressed in movies: Not the schlumpy alcoholic kind with a penchant for burying themselves in their work; more the Gregory Peck type in a pressed suit, filing a story from a far-flung location.

Ken looked up to see the waiter approaching the table, but before he could get his bearings, Lillian ordered for the two of them, going so far as to choose a side for him when the waiter revealed that the fish of the day came with either saffron rice or shoestring potatoes.

He opened his mouth to say something but a simmering rage bubbled up, constricting his throat. He felt it spread across his chest and travel down his arms. He gripped the salad fork and stuffed his other hand into his pocket. He envisioned himself rising from the table, carefully refolding his napkin and in no uncertain terms telling *LillianKnowsBest* to stuff it.

Instead he said, "I would have preferred the fries."

"The rice pairs better. Trust me. Besides, you're Oriental. Don't you like rice?" Lillian said, reaching for the bread basket. But her hand shook and she accidentally knocked over the candle and dropped the basket, sending the rolls tumbling into her lap. "Oh, Christ!" she swore, picking up the rolls and tipping over her cane in the process. "Oh, Geez! Pick that up, will you?"

Ken leaned over to pick up the cane but once his head was down and obscured by the table, a certain feeling took over. With the hands of a magician he withdrew his lighter and lit the edge of the tablecloth on fire. He watched the flames quickly lick up Lillian's side of the table. It was a deft move as it looked as if the toppled candle had caused the blaze. The next few minutes were a jumble. Lillian screamed and struggled to move from her chair while the waiter rushed over with a pitcher of water. The shock of the chain of events set off something in Lillian. Her body went rigid and then began to shake.

Other diners were up now, gathered around her chair, trying to gently lower her to the floor and dialing for help. A tall man with thinning hair stepped in to take charge. He looked familiar to Ken. Had the man done his taxes? No, that wasn't it. Worked at the library? No. A podiatrist? Yes, yes. That was it. He had given him a steroid injection for his plantar fasciitis a few years back and in a monotone world-weary way told him to pick up some inserts at the drugstore. The man seemed to come alive tonight, though.

"I'm a doctor!" he proclaimed, ripping off his jacket, folding it into a neat cushion, and placing it under Lillian's head. He gently placed his palms on either side of her head, informed the crowd that she was having a seizure and asked everyone to step back and give her some room. Ken backed away and receded into the crowd like an actor exiting backstage. His part was done. He passed the bus boy. He passed the hostess. He passed the paramedics in the parking lot.

Back home, he lit a fire and made himself a hot buttered rum. Rain began to fall and he paced back and forth; the cats circled him thinking it was a game. He took out his knitting, tossing the ball of multi-color yarn Jonathan had given him to the cats. He sat in contemplation of his early morning paddle on the kayak a few days ago. The way the mist hovered above the water. The way the striated sky was punctuated in soft puffs like kitten paws. The way the water reflected the flight pattern of the storm petrel. It made him think of the Arvo Pärt piece: *Speigel im Speigel*. Mirror in mirror. He put on the CD. As music filled the room, he began to carefully plan out his stitches, to lay out the different skeins in all the gradations of grey he had seen that morning on the water. It would be a tight intricate gorgeous knit.

Carole Symer
LANDING AT LAGUARDIA AIRPORT, YOU REMEMBER YOUR FATHER'S PSYCHOSIS

You say it was like yesterday:
the gods of the liver & blood arrive.

An old man stands over a sink
washing boxers in straight bleach.

The shell of a brute who once twisted
bread tags to birds' ankles.

Then, as if Baldy himself sprouted wings,
he shrugged & flew to paradise, no longer pretend.

You say it was night & you, a pale-faced boy
cannot hold a candle still.

I am so sorry the Hudson looks like dirt this time of year
as the plane leans left & circles to land.

You want to fall apart like clouds,
then sudden rain.

You carry it with you: the memory, some magic,
the life suspended in mid-air with him.

Yet here you are, my darling, a man who feels
it all & that boy no longer floating & weightless.

Ellen Stone
WOLF MOON OVER M-14

A rush of trucks waterfall
    the morning with a roar
        not unlike the rapids

of a river. Meanwhile,
    the moon's gaze is
        dogged through tree

limbs rooted in naked sky.
    Once I heard coyotes
        call in Saginaw Forest

that frigid grip of howl
    and yip, opened raw
        their echoed rounds.

Here the Wolf moon
    stuck fast over snowy roofs
        of sleeping houses. I wonder

what our yonder has
    become. Why we still
        hold on to this badge

of yellow-gold in early air.
    And, keen to hear
        something calling us, yearning

over the ridge, even
    though we know there is
        really nowhere left to go.

Catherine Turnbull
DUST

The things I have inherited
are growing dusty.
Crystal glasses, etched and dainty,
tea cups from another age, boxes
of letters in your first language,
paper albums full of faces
I never met. Necklaces,
silver, or not.
Though I try to protect them,
I cannot protect them from that.

Terry Bohnhorst Blackhawk
AT THE NATIONAL GALLERY OF ART: MEMORIAL VIEW
for N.P.F. (1939-2019)

To reach the Rothkos, climb four flights up,
past the Calder floating in light from windows
angled above the terrazzo staircase. Marble bright,
marble light: trilobites and shells embedded
underfoot, and on I go, my river's shores
opening out. I've passed the Bellows you loved,
Hughie Lee-Smith's ghetto flute ascending.

First stop, Magritte: a curtained emptiness.
Next, Max Ernst's "Moment of Calm" belies its name
with a textural busy-ness you'd have defied
these new motion sensors to peer into. I imagine you
imbibing this forest of drowned roller coasters, sgraffito
birds, bristlecone pines, collapsible cups un-collapsing
upward. You always did like to come nose-close.

In my wallet, a profile cut-out: you, hands
thrust deep in your painting smock, face tilting up,
lips puckered for a kiss—the photo just one
of many surprises you'd tuck into a pocket
or sock drawer after one of our weekends together.
You may never find this, you wrote on one,
but I hope it brings you joy if you do.

So when I arrive at the Rothkos and start writing
and a stranger interrupts to tell me I'm his "muse,"
I startle. He is so not you, yet I go on, into the Not-you now,
blab about Twombley, "art pilgrimages"— but why
talk to him at all? I sought a chapel. Not this.
The black square floats inside the maroon, the red above
                        the white. None (*all!*) of it is still.

Corinna Schulenburg
SUMMER IS

inspired by Ana Leovy's painting of the same name

Boy, I spy you
among the peaches and pears
an orchard fire

how you dangle that
cigarette, like death is just
one more thing to press

between lips.
I see your stripes, how they stretch
your body like a picnic

blanket for me to lay
my whole self down. Listen,
frisbees buzz the air

like swollen dragonflies.
Listen, summer has her plans
for us but she won't say.

I'll say this.
Yesterday the grass asked
for water, now feel how wet

the sky left her.
I don't believe in morals
but I'm fond of invitations

and consequences.
Boy, right now, your hand could ask
for what it wants

and the whole damn sky
might say yes, might say it
again, the way all these peaches

and pears keep falling
into the ripeness of our laps
like there is no full.

Jeffrey Hermann
I GET THAT REFLECTED LIGHT KEEPS GOING, BUT EXPLAIN AGAIN ABOUT ABSORBED LIGHT

Because I imagine a glow
inside unknowingly
like water comes and goes

You look at me
and where does that go

I'm walking around
the house collecting
things left behind

There are crumbs even
after I wipe the counter

Where do they go
the people we love
when they leave the house

Who thought to build
a particle collider

and smash small things
together that break apart

instead of joining together
like snowflakes

I'm sentimental
for anything beautiful

that touches the skin
of my children

what holds
a moment
dissolves

Where are you off to
today I asked her

She said today I'm slipping
into my pretty coat

and heading outside
to catch a little sun

Katie Hartsock
RETURNED

after *Indiana Jones and the Last Crusade*

The moment the meteor hit Michigan,
my son, not yet one, had just thrown a toy down
hard, with a delight so adamant he growled.

The earth shook, lamps flickered, and I stared like one
of myth's mortal mothers, one who delivered
a demi-god to cross the ground's soft grasses

and crush them, one who cannot but does believe,
and slightly fears, his power. These early feats
of strength break our hearts, this bright and early proof

our boys belong beyond us. And their fathers,
always in the next room, or realm — never there
to see thunderbolts light up little muscles.

Not much later I learned what really hit us.
As in the scene where Indiana, searching
for his father, locates the spot in the floor

of a library, once a church, he must smash
open. He unclips a stanchion, starts to bang
as the lone librarian stamps books returned,

and their blows coincide, every time. A gag,
and a minor heroic exploit, except
Indy will never know how he eluded

an outraged librarian, with Einstein hair
and delicate spectacles, who instead paused,
puzzled, at clangs that came, it seemed, from his hand.

Was he the golden child, after all?
His the supernatural force just now endowed,
given late in life, yet given nonetheless?

He regards the godhead latent in his stamp,
which brims with lengthy journeys he may be asked
to hazard. And sets it firmly, gently, down.

Karly Vance
MAGPIE

Distracted by light
They say; a fool
For colors. And yet—

In a slick of ice, in a pane
Of glass, in a sliding door,
In a wide black puddle

You see your body:
Sometimes speeding,
A dotted line in the sky,
Sometimes still as snow,

And you know.
The image is no visitor.
You are bound like a wound

By the wisdom to
Warn, to tell fortunes,
To play and to grieve,

To see the plank
In your own eye,
To know how to
Call, and call, and call,

And, in the end, to leave.

Mckensey Kendall
PEN PALS WITH PLUTO

You and I were standing barefoot on a piece of plywood
beneath a saturated twilight.

A still wheat field and a rusted Chevy in its middle,
the crickets screamed in between our quiet breaths.
I could feel them raging into the ether — vibrating with magic.
We must have been the last humans awake.

You looked like a little human then.
I could make out the contours of your face;
the pits from your acne scars and the bump on the bridge of your nose
were both upturned towards the moon.
The sky had opened just for us and in its vastness
I could see the hand that was supposed to feed us reaching down to eat.

To look up at you was to look at the constellations above;
to hold your little human body was to hold onto oblivion
and bury my face in its gossamer. You told me you wanted
to bond our atoms so we fused our bodies together
by the fingertips.

This year I learned what Death was;
this year I learned that strong bones snap the loudest.
I haven't met a corpse that hasn't looked just like you.
In your absence,
the stars outside and
the quiet inevitability of rotting
are the only things that I can anchor to.
Write me your letters in the constellations,
will you?

Keith Taylor
IN MEMORY

Great horned owls have not returned
to the heron rookery, sixteen clumps
of sticks woven high into the oaks
on a small island in a small lake.
For three decades my friend counted
the owls nesting there until herons
returned in spring to claim their place.

My friend can't remember the lake,
its oaks, its herons or its owls,
so I return midwinter, crunching
over the ice to check for owl-sign.
For five years now, the January nests
have held nothing but snow.

Theodore Deppe
LENINGRAD SYMPHONY

Horizontal rain at the windows and pulsatile tinnitus
pounding in my ears as I sit in the waiting room, apart
     from the other patients,

and try to read an essay on Shostakovich
(he says, *Every artist who isolates himself from the world is
     doomed*).

Though he wanted to finish the Seventh Symphony in his
     besieged city,
the State evacuated him, so the final score was spirited

back to Leningrad in a small plane over German lines,
     bringing with it
the problem of finding enough living musicians to play
     the massive work.

The radio offers a free trip for two to Tenerife
as I try to concentrate on the rehearsals
     during the Winter of Death:

a clarinetist whose reed was frozen and whose cracked lips
     couldn't produce a sound;
a cellist who arrived after burying his wife, one of the
     hundred thousand who starved each month;

and a percussionist who was sent to the city's morgue,
     then found to be not
dead after all. *The Leningrad Symphony*. Practiced
     by an orchestra, formed from fragments.

Finally, half-starved musicians performed it in August 1942,
     some wearing gloves
on their bone hands with holes cut for fingers.

Music broadcast through ruined streets, out to the enemy.
By the time Doctor Alex summons me, the tinnitus--small
      scourge

in the fabric of things but one that keeps me up at night--
has, of course, disappeared. Monica sets up a 24-hour
      blood pressure test

and every fifteen minutes, after the cuff inflates and I've
      let it read
me, I jot down what I've been doing. The first note records

walking the White Strand during a break in the gale
      on the way home.
I meet no one. And revel in that solitude. Why am I so
      happy

not seeing anyone? Shostakovich again: *I find it incredible
that an artist should want to shut himself away.* But how
      to reconcile

the need for solitude with the necessity of solidarity
      with others?
The cuff tightens and knows me. Oh, give me enough time to
      myself and I'll try

to connect. In the afternoon, the Seventh Symphony.
By the window, a bowl with four narcissus bulbs, like
      onion domes

on an Orthodox cathedral in a war zone. How do
you practice Shostakovich an hour after burying
      your wife?

I'm getting used to the quarter-hour checks, but Annie
        looks nervous
each time the motor kicks on to tighten the cuff.

Night, now, and I sleep until 4. Then the whooshing
        sound
that mirrors the pulse at my wrist returns to trouble both ears.

I've been told humming can briefly banish tinnitus
        so I hum Shostakovich
until the drumming stops, then return to the essay: an orchestra
        formed from the rubble.

Survival first, but, granted that, the imperative of music.
Then I give myself to the rhythms and songlines of sleep.

Russ Capaldi
MIRACLE

I think of the ancient poetess, LI Ch'ing Chao.
Here, a lady draws one delicate foot
over the other and murmurs beneath her sleep.
I open the bedroom window.
Her hip and side, her draped arm are contoured
like sunrise hills. A breeze stirs
through the screen, lifts the hair
from her neck, like a small pine bough
that reveals a fragile clutch.

Years ago,
   in a tent
      on the Yellowstone
bears circled every night for a week,
but didn't once come closer.

James Owens
AS IF DIAGRAMMING HOW CELLOS DISTURB THE AIR

... music requires chains. –Bernadus Sylvestris

Fourteen branches of the fallen ash
arch above water, where the scooped
column of the trunk rests drowned near shore,
in the risen spate of ice-melt, and,
as the water parts at each interruption
in the dark surface, luminous ripples
describe turbulence around every branch
and interfere with other multiplying ripples,
to merge, break, and merge again, so
the wavelets are an intricate, involuting
lace of gleams that persists briefly, trailing
into the current below, until the cross-woven
lines of turbulence dampen and cancel out,
and the unmarked, black water flows on.

Joyce Schmid

BUT IT DOESN'T MEAN THAT I DON'T LOVE YOU ANYMORE

The dry stream-bed has filled with waterfalls.
Flowers are returning, white among the tiny leaves,
nor am I the same.
I am not cyclical like them.
Your consternation rumbles through the valley
when I tell you I am changed.
Your fix your eyes on a banana slug.
It doesn't seem to move
but gets from here to there.
Why is an egret standing on the grass, so still,
so distant from the bay,
as wild turkeys cross the greening field?
The shadow of a cloud has almost caught them,
and I try to warn them. They don't care.
They neither run nor fly away,
they stay and graze, while one last mallard
glides by on the lake,
the darkness passing over her.

Emma Karnes
FREEDOM

To live out a life on the fields with the elk. With the sky
pressing upon you my lack like a rock. Lover, I am not there.
I am not the first beast with her eyes spinning like globes,
I am not the rough heat of her mate, huffing at her rind,
I am not the rotted-gummed last beast, pawing ceaselessly
at a bird's grave. I would give you my hands at the first cry.
Your hopelessness, your tire, you belong to an order
of chimerical grief. Go, please go, with the droughts and
the feasts. Go where bodies surge before dying without me.

Sharon Oriel
POEM WITHOUT AN END

after Yehuda Amichai

Inside the haughty new museum
there is an ancient croft house.
Inside the croft house
is me.
Inside me
my heart.
Inside my heart
a museum.
Inside the museum
a croft house,
inside
me,
inside me
my heart,
inside my heart
a museum

Terry Bohnhorst Blackhawk
I GO TO THE MUSEUM WITHOUT YOU

Without you I sink,
cross-hatched, armless and awkward,
barely nosing into the light.

Dark Ice, by Blane de St. Croix

I remember the touch
of your foot on my foot
the breath of my breath
in the small of your back
us making of ourselves
one shimmering beast
pulsing and twining, twinning
and glossy, our metallic
sweating fusing us, not one
inch belonging to oneself
alone, in luscious loop-
iness we were spinning
spiral-like, like the twister
from the west that night
that passed us by

The Couple, by Louise Bourgeois

My lonely canoe —
did Homer know I'd linger like this,
dipping my net listlessly in the stream?
Is that why he washed these hills with lilac?

Playing a Fish, by Winslow Homer

I walk through Sol's maze
in the absence of your love.
The walls intersect, baffle

in the absence of your love.
No palette breaks the starkness.
His lines are all I see.
I grow dizzy. My ears ring.

Wall Drawing 335, by Sol Lewitt

It's lovely, but surely Innes knew
red scudding leaves imply a bloodied sky.
I need more than this sodden chiaroscuro.
You'd have painted scouring light.
Not this petulant air.

Autumn in Montclair, by George Innes

Cloaked in your absence,
blinded by this swirling tower
of light, I think I will never
recover from the storm of his hatred.
I missed the rockets and blue lights
that gave early warning, learned
too late he was like the Moon Cussers,
lurking on the shore in the dark
of the moon, flashing false lights
to lure steamers to their destruction
on the shoals. They took whatever
they could from the foundering
vessels, the way he stripped me.

Rockets and Blue Lights, by J. M. W. Turner

In my cell
24-7 light allows no respite
and from all around eyes peer in —
every hour on
the hour. Check! Check!
I am an object of study.

I must lie as you did
for hours on the floor
until somebody would come or call.

Them and Us, by ERRE

I am doing my best not to
        think of hats
the shaggy one   woven   tattered straw
        not to move
my feet in even the tiniest
shuffle   lest lines of milk   not
tears   spill over the edge
of the bowl and soak my long black
skirt. I'm not Vermeer's light-
drenched maid pouring milk
from a stoneware pitcher.
I can only *balance*   every
second with
        its liquid burden   now
forward   now back and I know
I will go on this way
doing my best not to think
corduroy
      and the river nowhere near.

Carrying the Milk, Blu-ray installation by Marina Abramovic

My eyes open under water —
    Come, crushed mint
    mindless of the years.
    Airs of summer passion
    lessen in the mowing,
    owing only breath,
    death the drying season.
    Reason picks a blossom,
    blesses what it can.

Hands off, wayward creature.
Nature finds us wanting,
haunting ancient wells.
Bells of woodland, ring,
sing us through the forest,
restore us, make us wholesome.
Come, crushed mint.
Kom hjärtans fröjd.

Fantasias Modulares, by Ad Minolfi

Once I fell into purple, now I am a receding shade of plum,
brownish, my face murky in retreat. I could be a saint, an icon,
looking down on these clueless flowers. It's as if all life belongs to
them now, blowzy songs erupting from the pitcher's ceramic lip.
But if I say *cosmos, carnations* or listen to the sly chime of that bud
just beginning to open, still there is a music to it, the small blue
cornflowers dancing on their own.

Woman with a Vase of Flowers, by Odilon Redon

Kom hjärtans fröjd (Come heart's delight), refrain from the
Swedish folksong *"Uti Vår Hage"* ("Out in Our Meadow").

Joe Sacksteder
SLOUGH OFF

First it must be dissected, desecrated.
Scrape it naked, leave it shivering and shamed,
a forced sloughing, exuvia flaking to the tarps below,
cloud of sawdust a blinding defense mechanism
achieving eyeballs and lungs
despite fogging goggles and sweat-drenched mask.
The house fights back; it can't see past this indignity
to the pride of future plumes.

The youngest on the crew, the brunt of every joke,
the mascot, the golden gofer — until today.
"Did you see the new guy?" standing dazed
at the base of the twenty-eight foot extension, scraper in hand,
wondering what I still wonder: how can these people
do this every day? The change is immediate, in me and at me,
suddenly scrambling to billy goat feats of precarity,
suddenly prone to more general idleness
interrupted by furious bouts of productivity
to show who's still the boss, relatively speaking;
"R, this is J. If J tells you to eat shit,
you eat shit."

In his eyes, my eyes: how can they stand
scraping a life from a shitty summer job?
Thirty, thirty-five, sixty — *this too will pass*
soon to be an epitaph. What keeps them here?
Me, and now R, new guys — hydra dynasty,
an endless audience to disbelieve their recalcitrance,
their ossification, to admire their expertise
in something very specific, to swipe eagerly at the dangled then
snatched away crew camaraderie, the shit-shooting,

until it's actually the old proving it to the young,
though the young must never know.

Luckily the tasks get progressively easier
— scrape, sand, caulk, paint —
as the living gets progressively harder.

1883, old for this country. We undo the labor
of forty, eighty, one hundred thirty years,
shed the sweat of some dead young man
reeling under the need for food, shelter,
the complications of girls and drinking.

We scrape off the last layers of old paint.
Underneath it all, fresh grain.

Art Curtis
CANOEING THE RAPIDS

Drop
over
the
lip
bow left
bow right
stern
turn
dip and pull

s
t
a
n
d
i
n
g
wave
bow left
bow right
stern
turn

dip and pull
to passage near bank

Below the rapids
lay paddle across thwart.
Wipe away sweat.
Let current point.
Listen for the thunder.
Back paddle;
reconnoiter,
look for a channel.

Drop
over
the
lip

bow right
dip and pull
bow left
paddle starboard.

Stern
s
w
i
n
g
s
toward rock.

Pull!!!
Pull!!!
Pull harder!!!

Paddle to port
dip and pull
dip and pull

bow left
bow right

stern
turn

dip and pull
paddle to port.

Pull hard again!

Breathe deeply.

CONTRIBUTOR BIOS

At age ten, a friend and *SHERRILL ALESIAK wrote stories about Elvis and Fabian, and her literary life began. She's grateful that her poetry or fiction has appeared in publications as *Alligator Juniper, The MacGuffin, Kalliope, Princeton Arts Review, The Owen Wister Review, Blueline, 34th Parallel* and the poetry anthology, *Eating Her Wedding Dress.*

DEBORAH ALLBRITAIN's poetry appears or is forthcoming in the *Beloit Poetry Journal, Ecotone,* and the *Potomac Review.* She received the Patricia Dobler Poetry Prize in 2017.

ESTELLE BAJOU's poetry is featured in *California Quarterly, Heavy Feather Review, Variant Literature,* and elsewhere. Her debut collection, *I Never Learned to Pray,* is forthcoming in 2022. Her poem, "Honour Thy Error as a Hidden Intention," from *This Broken Shore* (2021), is nominated for the Pushcart. www.estellebajou.com

A finalist for the Miller Williams poetry prize, ROY BENTLEY has published ten books. His work has appeared in *Dunes Review, Blackbird, Shenandoah, december, Crazyhorse, The Southern Review,* and *Prairie Schooner* among others. His latest book of poems, *Beautiful Plenty,* is out from Main Street Rag.

Founding Director of Detroit's InsideOut Literary Arts Project, *DR. TERRY BOHNHORST BLACKHAWK's five poetry collections include *Escape Artist* (BkMk Press), winner of the 2003 John Ciardi Prize, and *One Less River* (Mayapple Press), a Kirkus Reviews Best 2019 Poetry Title. She has won the Pablo Neruda Prize from *Nimrod* and a fellowship from Kresge Arts in Detroit.

CYNTHIA BOORUJY has been published in *Consequence Forum* and *Open Door Review.* She was one of several Los Angeles poets chosen for the 2021 public art project *Love Letters in Light.* She lives in Santa Monica, CA where she is working on her debut novel.

*RUSS CAPALDI lives with his wife in Petoskey, Michigan. He has poems in *Rosebud, Dunes Review, Appalachia,* and *North Dakota Quarterly.* He has published essays in *Traverse* magazine.

*DIANE CARR had an active life as an artist in Detroit where she exhibited her art and taught art at colleges in Detroit. She created an 18-foot-high steel outdoor sculpture, *Skystone,* for a Michigan Welcome Center. After working in a large downtown warehouse studio, she now has a studio in a northern Michigan woods and lives surrounded by the source of her art.

*ART CURTIS was writing ad copy when he turned to poetry in 1991 after reading Jim Harrison's *Letters to Yesenin* during a major personal crisis. He lives near Bellaire with Strider, a miniature Puma, and finds Petoskey stones in his sandy garden nearly 400 feet above Lake Michigan.

THEODORE DEPPE is the author of seven books of poems. His most recent collection is *Riverlight* (Arlen House, 2019). He lives in Connemara, Ireland.

*MICHELLE DEROSE lives in Grand Rapids, Michigan, where she teaches creative writing and African American, Irish, and world literature at Aquinas College. She and her husband take full advantage of their home state where they are avid bicyclists, canoeists, hikers, and campers.

SARA DUDO is a second-year MFA student and graduate assistant at University of Nevada Las Vegas. She just married her best friend in June and enjoys writing, running, and surfing. Her work has recently been published or forthcoming in *Tiny Journal, Bridge, Pine Row, Red Rock Review*, and others.

JENNIFER FANDEL's poetry has been published in *The American Journal of Poetry, Ginger, Measure, The Baltimore Review*, and *RHINO*, as well as a number of anthologies including *Hope Is the Thing: Wisconsinites on Hope and Resilience in the Time of Covid-19* (Wisconsin Historical Society Press). She teaches writing in prisons in Wisconsin.

*MERRITT GOLICK is a writer, teacher, and voracious reader based in Ferndale, Michigan. She works primarily in the genres of short fiction and poetry.

ROBIN GOW is a trans poet and young adult author from rural Pennsylvania. They are the author of *Our Lady of Perpetual Degeneracy* and the chapbook *Honeysuckle*. Their first YA novel, *A Million Quiet Revolutions*, is forthcoming March 2022 with FSG Books for Young Readers.

*KATIE HARTSOCK is the author of *Bed of Impatiens* (Able Muse Press). Recent poems appear in *Poetry, Threepenny Review, 32 Poems, Kenyon Review, Beloit Poetry Journal*, and elsewhere. She teaches at Oakland University in Michigan, where she lives with her husband and two young sons.

*JEFFREY HERMANN's poetry and prose has appeared in *Hobart, Palette Poetry, UCity Review, trampset, The Shore*, and other publications. Though less publicized, he finds his work as a father and husband to be rewarding beyond measure.

*MICHAEL HUGHES has written since high school, first inspired by Robert Frost and Emily Dickinson. He draws from nature, and the tragic, endearing things people do. Rooted in the soil of West Virginia, he now lives with his wife Janet in Benzie County, Michigan, which he also considers almost heaven.

*DANIELLE JOHNSON is a poet, band member, writing instructor, corporate sellout, biography reader, Grand Valley alum, Georgia College MFA graduate, and Michigan native. These accomplishments are nice but the greatest thing is the love and support she has from her spouse, her family, her friends, and her dog, Noodle.

EMMA KARNES is a graduate of the University of Virginia, where she studied poetry and is currently pursuing a Masters of Public Policy. She's been writing poetry ever since her second-grade teacher introduced her to acrostics and diamantes. Emma's work appears in *Rattle Young Poets Anthology*, *The Healing Muse*, *Tilde*, and elsewhere.

*MCKENSEY E. KENDALL is a young artist from Mesick, Michigan. She is currently working towards a Bachelor of Fine Arts at The School of the Art Institute of Chicago where she is focusing on painting.

*DEIRDRE MAHONEY's writing has appeared in *Multiplicity Magazine* and *The Boardman Review*. She is on the English faculty at Northwestern Michigan College in Traverse City.

*PAUL MAXBAUER, a retired history teacher, lives in Traverse City, Michigan. He now spends his time writing poems and short stories. He had a poem chosen for the *Poets Night Out 2019* chapbook by TADL, and another poem appeared in *Dunes Review*.

ALEXIS NEWTON is a freshman English major at UMASS Amherst. Her poetry has most recently been published in the *Matthew Wolfe Pandemic Evolution* anthology and *The Battering Ram Literary Journal*. Unsure of what the future holds, she plans to keep writing as long as she can.

*SHARON L. ORIEL is the author of *Lochan*, a handstitched chapbook in a limited edition of 50. *Hummingbird, Magazine of the Short Poem* and *Solitary Plover*, the newsletter of Lorene Niedecker, have published her poems. Sharon lives on the banks of the Crystal River in northwestern Michigan.

ANTHONY OTTEN lives in Kentucky. His short stories have won first prize in contests held by the journals *Still* and *Able Muse*. His writing has also appeared in *The Forge Literary Magazine*, *Jabberwock Review*, *Valparaiso Fiction Review*, and *Grasslimb Journal*. Find him @AnthonyOtten on Twitter and at anthonyotten.com.

JAMES OWENS' newest book is *Family Portrait with Scythe* (Bottom Dog Press, 2020). His poems and translations appear widely in literary journals, including recent or upcoming publications in *Grain, Dalhousie Review, Presence, Queen's Quarterly*, and *Honest Ulsterman*. He earned an MFA at the University of Alabama and lives in a small town in northern Ontario.

CHRISTINE PENNYLEGION has lived in and around Toronto, Ottawa, Pittsburgh, Baltimore, and Windsor. She holds a BA(Hons) in English from the University of Toronto, and an MAR from Trinity School for Ministry. Read more at christinepennylegion.com.

*TUULI QIN-TERRILL's poetry has appeared in or is forthcoming in the *Inflectionist Review*, *EXILE*, and *Halfway Down the Stairs*. She grew up in Traverse City and currently works as a biopharmaceutical lab analyst in Wisconsin.

BAILEY QUINN is currently pursuing her Master of Arts in English at Weber State University. Her work has appeared in *The Elevation Review*, *Rubbertop Review*, and *Open Minds Quarterly*. She holds a Bachelor of Arts in English from Brigham Young University.

*RON RIEKKI's books include *My Ancestors are Reindeer Herders and I Am Melting in Extinction* (Loyola University Maryland's Apprentice House Press), *Posttraumatic* (Hoot 'n' Waddle), and *U.P.* (Ghost Road Press). Right now, Riekki's listening to Dr. Shelly Harrell's "Healing Racial Stress and Trauma."

*JOE SACKSTEDER is the author of the short story collection *Make/Shift* (Sarabande Books) and the novel *Driftless Quintet* (Schaffner Press). Recent publications include *The Offing, Salt Hill, Ninth Letter, Denver Quarterly*, and *New South*. He is a PhD candidate at the University of Utah and Director of Creative Writing at Interlochen Center for the Arts.

JOYCE SCHMID's most recent work appears or is forthcoming in *Five Points, Northwest Review, Poetry East, Literary Imagination*, and other journals and anthologies. She lives with her husband of over half a century in Palo Alto, California.

CORINNA SCHULENBURG (she/her) is an artist/activist committed to ensemble practice and social justice. She's a white queer transgender woman, a mother, a playwright, a poet, and a founding Creative Partner of Flux Theatre Ensemble. She has poems upcoming in *Canned, Capsule, Eclectica, Oroboro*, and *LUPERCALIA*. https://corinnaschulenburg.com/

*HOLLY WREN SPAULDING is the author of *Familiars* and *Between Us* from Alice Greene & Company. St. Brigid Press published her chapbook *Fire* in 2021. Her essay, "The Language of Trees," was included in *Elemental: A Collection of Michigan Creative Nonfiction* (Wayne State University Press, 2018). www.hollywrenspaulding.com

*ELLEN STONE advises a poetry club at Community High School in Ann Arbor, Michigan and is a co-host of Skazat, a monthly poetry series in Ann Arbor, Michigan. She is the author of *What Is in the Blood* (Mayapple Press, 2020) and *The Solid Living World* (Michigan Writers' Cooperative Press, 2013).

*ALISON SWAN"s fifth book, *A Fine Canopy*, was named one of the eleven most anticipated poetry releases of fall 2020 by Literary Hub. Her first, *Fresh Water: Women Writing on the Great Lakes*, is a Michigan Notable Book. She is a Mesa Refuge alum and Petoskey Prize for Environmental Leadership co-winner.

*CAROLE SYMER is a psychologist in Ann Arbor and teaches at New York University. Her writing has appeared in *Across the Margin, Black Fox Literary*

Magazine, Mutha Magazine, Sky Island Journal, Wild Roof Journal, and *Michigan Chronicle.* She's the 2020 recipient of the Oomen & Schultz Interlochen Writing Scholarship. Her chapbook, *Glint,* was released in 2021 from Small Harbor Publishing.

KELLY TALBOT has edited books and other content for twenty years for *Wiley, Macmillan, Oxford, Pearson Education,* and other publishers. His writing has appeared in dozens of magazines and anthologies. He divides his time between Indianapolis, Indiana, and Timisoara, Romania.

Over the years *KEITH TAYLOR has published widely in North America and Europe. His most recent full-length collection of poetry was *The Bird-while* (Wayne State University Press, 2017). After working as a bookseller for a couple of decades, he taught for a few years in the writing programs at the University of Michigan.

*KATHLEEN TIGHE is a writer and educator based in Michigan. She writes primarily creative nonfiction, flash fiction, and poetry. Her work has appeared in *Still Life, Qua Literary and Fine Arts Magazine,* and *Writing From the Inside Out.* Her passion for traveling has informed her view of our fleeting time on planet Earth and influences much of her work.

*CATHERINE TURNBULL's poetry has appeared in *Tupelo Quarterly, Ruminate, Dos Passos Review,* and others. She is the author of a 2008 chapbook, *The Chocolatier Speaks of His Wife.* A manuscript-in-progress, *The Spider's Apprentice,* was twice a finalist for the Dorset Prize at Tupelo Press. She lives and works in Traverse City, MI.

*KARLY VANCE grew up in Bay City, Michigan and studied writing at Hope College. Her writing has been published in *The Offbeat, Common Ground Review, Midwest Quarterly,* and *Madison Review.* She currently lives with her husband and son in the Chicago area.

Tucked deep in the Northern Michigan wilderness, *MAGGIE MENEZES WALCOTT lives with her family in a house they built themselves. Her pieces have been published in *Every Day Fiction, Trouvaille Review, Last Leaves Magazine, Dillydoun Review* and *Mothers Always Write,* among others.

NATALIE WELBER is an actor, playwright, and poet based in Chicago, IL. Her poetry has been recently published or is forthcoming in *Sheila-Na-Gig, Not Very Quiet,* and *a* You can find more at nataliewelber.com. She dedicates these poems to San.

CLAYNE ZOLLINGER III was born and raised in Idaho, but currently resides in Oakland, California. He received his MFA in Creative Writing from Saint Mary's College of California. His poems have appeared in *Talking River.*

READER BIOS

*KELLI FITZPATRICK is an author and editor from Michigan. Her fiction has been published by Simon and Schuster, *Flash Fiction Online*, and *Crazy 8 Press*, among others, and her poetry appears in *Dunes Review*, *Still Life*, and *KYSO Flash*. She has written and edited for the *Star Trek Adventures* game line from Modiphius. She is an advocate for the arts, public education, and gender rights and representation. Connect at KelliFitzpatrick.com and on Twitter @KelliFitzWrites.

*CHRISTOPHER GIROUX received his doctorate from Wayne State University and is a professor of English at Saginaw Valley State University, where he has served as faculty advisor for the school's literary magazine and co-founded the community arts journal *Still Life*. His second chapbook, *Sheltered in Place*, is scheduled to be published in 2022.

*PAUL OH is an aspiring writer and editor. He is currently finishing his undergraduate degree in Creative Writing at Colorado College. You can find him anxiously working on his thesis novel, which, at last check, is almost halfway done.

*TERESA SCOLLON is the author of *Trees and Other Creatures* (Alice Greene, 2021), *To Embroider the Ground with Prayer* (Wayne State University Press), and a chapbook from Michigan Writers Cooperative Press. Her essay "Earth" was included in *Elemental*, an anthology of Michigan essayists. A National Endowment for the Arts fellow, she teaches the Writers Studio program at North Ed Career Tech in Traverse City.

*When EMMA SMITH was in middle school, teachers said she was having difficulty reading. As her worried parents contemplated purchasing Hooked on Phonics, Emma picked up *IT* by Stephen King and hasn't slowed down since. She loves to read everything from sci fi/fantasy to outdated anarchist literature to the classics. You can find Emma working with animals, reading books, or hiking with friends.

*JENNIFER YEATTS' literary life has included MA and MFA degrees in poetry, teaching writing in various forms, and editorial roles at *Passages North* and *Fugue*. She is the director of coffee for Higher Grounds Trading Company.

*denotes Michigan native or resident

SUBMISSION GUIDELINES

Dunes Review welcomes work from writers, artists, and photographers at all stages of their careers living anywhere in the world, though we particularly love featuring writers with ties to Michigan and the Midwest. We are open to all styles and aesthetics, but please read the following paragraph carefully to dive a little deeper into what we're looking for.

Ultimately, we're looking for work that draws us in from the very first line: with image, with sound, with sense, with lack of sense. We're looking for writing that makes us *feel* and bowls us over, lifts us up, and takes us places we've never been to show us ordinary things in ways we've never seen them. We're looking for poems and stories and essays that teach us how to read them and pull us back to their beginnings as soon as we've read their final lines. We're looking for things we can't wait to read again, things we can't wait to share with the nearest person who will listen. Send us your best work. We'll give it our best attention.

Submissions are accepted only via our Submittable platform: www.dunesreview.submittable.com. We do not consider work sent through postal mail or email. Any submissions sent through email will not be read or responded to. Please see further guidelines posted on our site. We look forward to reading your work!

Call for Patrons

Dunes Review is a not-for-profit endeavor to promote creative work within the Northern Michigan writing community and beyond.

The cost of publication can be underwritten in part by individual contributions.
We invite you to support the publication of the next issue with a donation of $25.

Send your check payable
to **Michigan Writers** to:

Michigan Writers
P.O. Box 2355
Traverse City, MI 49685

Thank you in advance for your support!

Made in USA - Kendallville, IN
77359_9781950744077
01.28.2022 1503